The Homeowner's
Property Tax Relief

The Homeowner's Property Tax Relief Kit

Lawrence J. Czaplyski
Vincent P. Czaplyski

McGraw-Hill, Inc.
New York   St. Louis   San Francisco   Auckland   Bogotá
Caracas   Lisbon   London   Madrid   Mexico   Milan
Montreal   New Delhi   Paris   San Juan   São Paulo
Singapore   Sydney   Tokyo   Toronto

Library of Congress Cataloging-in-Publication Data

Czaplyski, Lawrence J.
    The homeowner's property tax relief kit / Lawrence J. Czaplyski,
Vincent P. Czaplyski.
        p.   cm.
    Includes bibliographical references.
    ISBN 0–07–015069-9 :   — ISBN 0–07–015070-2:   (pbk.)
    1. Real property tax—Law and legislation—United States—Popular
works.   2. Tax assessment—Law and legislation—United States—
Popular works.   3. Tax protests and appeals—United States—Popular
works.   I. Czaplyski, Vincent P.   II. Title.
KF6760.Z9C93 1992
343.7305'4—dc20
[347.30354]   92-6381
                                                    CIP

1 2 3 4 5 6 7 8 9 0   DOH/DOH   9 8 7 6 5 4 3 2

ISBN 0-07-015069-9
ISBN 0-07-015070-2 {PBK}

The sponsoring editor for this book was Caroline Carney, the editing
supervisor was Fred Dahl, and the production supervisor was Donald F.
Schmidt. It was set in Palatino by Inkwell Publishing Services.

Printed and bound by R. R. Donnelley & Sons Company.

To our parents, Lawrence and Eileen,
for always being there for us.

Contents

Introduction

This book was written to help you save money on your property taxes. If you are like most homeowners, you've seen your taxes spiraling steadily upward in recent years. Each year's tax bill is always larger than the last. It can get very frustrating.

Now you can do something about it.

Using this book, you can determine if your tax assessment is fair and equitable. If it isn't, you'll find out how to successfully challenge your assessment to win a permanent tax reduction.

A successful appeal can save you hundreds of dollars. And those hundreds of dollars can be saved each and every year you own your home.

Besides saving money, you'll make sure that you are not paying more than your fair share of the property tax burden. Each state attempts to ensure that property taxes fall equally on every property owner's shoulders. But for a number of reasons (which we explain), it's difficult, if not impossible, to guarantee fairness. Many homeowners end up paying more than their fair share of the tax load. Only a small percentage of these homeowners appeal their assessments, yet a significant number of those who do, receive a reduction in their tax bill. This book shows you how to reduce your tax bill by taking you step by step through the assessment process. It includes worksheets and completed examples to guide you in analyzing your home's tax assessment. Here's what you'll find inside:

Chapter 1, "A Tale of Two Taxpayers," tells the story of Sara and Robert, two homeowners in an average neighborhood. Sara learns the rules of the property tax system game and plays to win. Robert pays the price of ignorance—more taxes than he really owes.

Chapter 2, "Assessing Real Property and Determining the Tax Rate," shows you how a municipality goes about assessing property and computing the tax rate. It defines assessed value, introduces the tax assessor, and shows how the assessor goes about the business of assessing properties (your house among them). It introduces the three traditional means of valuing property and explains which methods are preferred for valuing residential property.

Chapter 3, "Grounds for Challenging Your Property Tax Assessment," examines the major reasons for unfair property tax assessments. It focuses on three areas: mechanical errors, valuation errors, and legal errors. You'll learn exactly how to find these same kinds of errors in your property's value assessment.

Chapter 4, "The Assessor's Office and Beyond," describes what to expect when you visit the assessor's office. It looks at the assessor, at how the assessor's office operates, and at the resources available for the taxpayer considering an appeal.

Chapter 5, "The Cost Approach," explores in detail the cost approach to valuing residential property. You'll learn the strengths and weaknesses of this approach and why assessors often favor it. Several detailed examples provide you with a sound understanding of this important means of valuing property.

Chapter 6, "The Market-Data Approach," examines the market-data, or comparable sales, approach to valuing residential property. By example, you will be guided through the three main steps of this process, including just how to adjust the sale prices of comparable properties.

Chapter 7, "Property Tax Exemptions," discusses these often excellent sources of tax reductions. It defines some common exemptions and explains how typical eligibility requirements are established.

Chapter 8, "Organizing Your Tax Appeal," demonstrates the best ways to organize and present your appeal to the assessor. It details each step needed to create a powerful appeal, and includes two complete examples, one involving a single family home and the other a condominium.

Chapter 9, "Go Ask the Assessor," presents advice from assessors from around the country about how residential taxpayers can ensure the accuracy of their assessments and present the best appeal of an assessment to the assessor. They tell what they like and dislike, and how you can avoid some common stumbling blocks in presenting an appeal.

Chapter 10, "Meeting with the Assessor or Appeal Board," tells you what you need to know for that all-important meeting with the assessor or appeal board. It provides summaries of numerous actual tax appeal board cases, emphasizing the main issues involved and the reasoning behind each board's ultimate decision.

Chapter 11, "California—A Unique Case," explores the aspects of California property taxation that make it unique and different from the rest of the country.

In the appendices, we provide you with important property tax information for each state, along with many useful checklists and forms that will help you organize your own tax and property information.

We think you'll find everything you need within these pages to determine if your assessment is fair, and how to challenge it successfully if it is not.

Acknowledgments

We would like to thank the numerous persons who took time to respond to our requests for help in preparing this book. In particular, we would like to thank the many assessors from around the country who graciously offered insight into their profession.

Thanks also to Marshall & Swift for permission to reprint sections of the *Residential Cost Handbook* in Chap. 5.

And thanks to our wives and children, for their patience.

Lawrence J. Czaplyski
Vincent P. Czaplyski

A Tale of Two Taxpayers

*Next to the right of liberty, the right of
property is the most improtant individual
right guaranteed by the Constitution and the
one which, united with that of personal
liberty, has contributed more to the growth
of civilization than any other institution
established by the human race.*
WILLIAM HOWARD TAFT (1857–1930),
American president

Why a book on property taxation? Consider the following tale of two taxpayers,
Sara and Robert. Like most people, each wants a nice affordable place to live and
each is willing to work hard to get it. Their homes are in a good neighborhood of
similar sized, Cape Cod style homes. In fact, they live across from each other on
the same tree lined street. Their mortgage payments are similar and each lives on
about the same amount of income.

Sara and Robert share many similarities in their existence, but awareness of the
local property taxation system is not one of them. Sara, being more inquisitive
than Robert, makes it a point to learn how and why her home is taxed. She knows
that her home's value has something to do with the amount of taxes she pays, so
she decides to find out just how the town assessor determines the taxable value
for her home.

Sara's investigations uncover all kinds of interesting facts that affect, in the end,
just how much money she pays to the town in property taxes every year. Robert is
blissfully unaware that there is anything he can do to affect the ever rising tax bill
he receives like clockwork each spring.

Sara starts out by gathering all the information she can from her local assessor's
office. She applies for, and receives from the town assessor, a partial exemption
from payment of her property taxes. The town has approved various tax exemptions for residents, including one for those who install certain energy efficient
features in their homes, like the solar heating panels nearly everyone on the street
(including Robert) has purchased. Although the $100 she saves each year because
of this is not a large amount, it is free for the asking.

Robert is unaware of this exemption and so he does nothing about applying for
it. He continues to needlessly pay the extra money on his tax bill.

A quick review of the property records at the assessing office reveals several obvious mistakes to Sara. For some reason the former assessor has listed the lot size of her property as 24,000 ft^2. In actuality it is only 14,000 ft^2 and the new assessor has not gotten around to verifying the figures. In addition, Sara notes that the town's records show she is being taxed on an inground swimming pool. In fact she once applied for a building permit for a pool, but changed her mind and cancelled the project.

She puts together some well documented evidence to support her claim that her home is too highly assessed. She presents her evidence to the assessor during the annual period for tax abatement applications. Not surprisingly, she wins her claim and realizes significant tax savings.

And what of Robert? Besides not taking advantage of the solar heating exemption, he misses out on other tax savings as well. The town records contain a significant uncorrected mistake in the description of his property. In all, Robert pays nearly $600 more in property taxes per year than he should. And just as Sara's tax savings accrue every year, Robert's unnecessary losses continue to pile up.

Sara and Robert are imaginary, but their real life counterparts can be found in every neighborhood, large and small, in America. The millions of property owners in this country must all deal with a complex and far from perfect, several-centuries-old property taxation system. This system contains any number of ways in which individual property owners may be treated inequitably. *Mechanical errors* like the incorrect records of land or house dimensions in our example are just one of the numerous kinds of assessment mistakes that can result in unfair tax burdens.

As we shall see, there are other property tax gremlins lurking around out there, just waiting to inflate your tax bill. Fortunately, though, you can send every one of them packing by being like Sara, just a little bit assertive. All you need to do is learn how the property taxation system works and decide to use this knowledge.

Today in this country more people like Sara are asserting themselves when it comes to property taxes. A true taxpayer revolt has been underway since 1978 when Proposition 13 was passed in California. Proposition 13 was among the first popular state referendums to limit the growth of property taxes. It was a clear cut vote of no confidence in the ability of politicians to overhaul a runaway property-tax system themselves. By the beginning of the nineties the revolt has spread nearly everywhere in the country. In all but a handful of states, there is now some sort of statutory limit on the relative amount of property taxes that may be assessed against a residential property. Massachusetts' Proposition 2½ is another example of such legislation and more such enactments will almost certainly occur.

Despite winning many of these property-tax battles, the war is far from won for property owners, and in localities across the nation property taxes continue to rise. In 1982 for example, localities collected an average of about $3.26 in property taxes for every $100 of property value. By 1988 that figure had changed to $3.51 per $100 of value, an over 8 percent increase. During the period from 1989 through 1991, 87 percent of municipalities raised real estate tax rates by an average of 24 percent.

In some parts of the country increases during the same period have been on the order of 100 percent or more. In New York City today, the owner of a one to three family dwelling pays nearly *$10 per $100 of value*, or almost 10 percent of the home's value in property taxes.

America's rising indignation with high property taxes is evident in a yearly Gallup Organization poll of taxpayer sentiment commissioned by the Advisory Commission on Intergovernmental Relations. It asks taxpayers what they feel is the worst of all taxes. In 1989, for the first time in eleven years, property taxes were voted the worst of all taxes, even more onerous than federal income taxes. Today, in fact, a good number of property owners pay more in property taxes than they do in federal income taxes.

The property-tax burden will almost certainly continue to worsen before it gets better. In 1991 a record number of states were unable to pass budgets by the statutory deadlines. For the first time in the history of our nation, towns and cities are openly considering filing for Chapter 11 bankruptcy protection. Why? Among the complex set of problems facing municipalities everywhere is the undeniable reality that much of the federal funding relied upon by states and municipalities in the past is no longer available, attributed in large measure to Reagan Administration tax cuts.

The intrigue of insider Washington political maneuvering can seem far removed from our everyday life, but the effects of these funding cuts has been immediately and directly felt around the nation. Less federal aid to states means less state aid to towns and cities. Congress compounds the problem by continuing to enact legislation requiring state and local governments to fix a multitude of problems but does not supply federal money to assist them. Municipalities, more and more, face a choice between service cutbacks or increased property taxes, and often must choose both. Individual taxpayers, the bottom of the tax "food chain," are where the buck stops, and are expected to make up the shortfalls in revenue.

Today, it is these individual taxpayers who are taking it upon themselves, more than ever before, to verify the accuracy and fairness of their tax assessments. Some are braving the system unassisted, while a growing number have hired property-tax consultants, lawyers, and accountants to navigate the sometimes murky waters for them.

And it is for you, the individual taxpayer, that this book has been written. No matter what statutory limits are placed on property taxes in your hometown, or what the politicians promise, ultimately it is the fairness of the tax assessment on your home or condominium which matters most to you. This book will show you how to tell if your property taxes are equitable, and if they are not, how to prepare the very best arguments favoring a lower tax assessment.

If this is your first encounter with the property-tax bureaucracy (and it is a bureaucracy), take heart. By one estimate, only a tiny fraction of all property owners ever bother to apply for a tax abatement or refund of excess property taxes, but a large majority of those who do so receive an abatement.

How did the property taxation system in America come to be? Why does it sometimes let mistakes large and small go undetected? Why hasn't it changed to suit the times? More importantly, how can you avoid the pitfalls that befell Robert and learn to be more like Sara? In Chap. 2 we'll look at how property is assessed and how tax rates are determined.

Assessing Real Property and Determining the Tax Rate

There's millions in it.
    MARK TWAIN, *The Gilded Age* (1873)

The purpose of this chapter is to explain how the assessment and taxing of real property works. You are probably familiar with the taxation part, or at least the part where the tax bill comes in the mail and you have to pay it. But much of the rest of the assessing and taxing process is confusing, to the point where it seems almost deliberately so.

One of the reasons for this is the immense number of taxing jurisdictions in the United States today (almost 70,000). All these towns, villages, school boards, cities, sewer districts, fire districts, and counties each must keep track of countless properties and records. Many of these jurisdictions have differing rules, forms, and deadlines for doing this. And where there is some similarity of rules, there are different individuals interpreting the rules. The majority of these individuals are competent and hard working; however, they may be buried under a deluge of data they cannot cope with because they can't afford modern tools or their staffs are too small.

Another reason for this confusion is that many of the taxing jurisdictions just aren't taxpayer friendly. Forms and informational brochures are typically complicated and difficult to comprehend. Some offices are understaffed and simply do not have the resources to offer clear, useful help to taxpayers.

But the process of assessing and taxing real property can be understood. What follows is a description that is designed to give you a good, basic understanding of the assessment and taxation process.

In order to tax property according to its value, one must first be able to determine, with some accuracy, what that value is. Not coincidentally perhaps, acceptance of an ad valorem basis for taxation of property occurred as methods of valuing property became more formalized. By the nineteenth century, several ways of determining the value of real estate had developed, and they are still in use today in essentially the same forms. They are known as the income, the cost, and the market data approaches or methods. This chapter contains an overview of these methods of valuing property.

What Is Property?

So far we have briefly seen how property taxation came to be in the United States. But just what is property? It's easy to look at an acre of land and say with certainty that it is the 43,560 ft^2 of land bounded by that stream and this fence. Its location would then be unmistakable, and we would have described the physical *real estate*. However, a larger point would be missed. Property is more precisely defined by the *rights* a person may enjoy in relation to the physical "thing" that is the property.

Let's take the acre of land for example. As the owner, you enjoy certain privileges in relation to this land that are not afforded to others. You may decide to use it for a specific legal purpose, or you may decide to sell it. You may decide to do nothing at all with it, or you might decide to give it to a favorite nephew for a wedding gift. Over decades or centuries, as ownership of the acre shifts among individuals, the physical land (the real estate) may stay the same but the rights associated with it will have moved from one person to another, or to many others at one time. The acre's physical boundaries describe where it is, but the rights attached to it define the property's value to the owner and others. *Real property* is the total collection of rights associated with a particular piece of real estate.

Over the centuries, property rights have been debated in the courts of this and other countries. In particular, the English system of common law has contributed greatly to American legal notions of property rights and ownership. Today we speak of the *bundle of rights* to describe all of the possible rights associated with a piece of property.

The bundle of rights has been likened to a bundle of sticks, each representing one particular property right. The six basic property rights contained in the bundle are:

> The right to enter upon or leave.
>
> The right to use in any legal fashion.
>
> The right to sell.
>
> The right to rent or lease.
>
> The right to give away.
>
> The right to not do any of these.

As owner, you may transfer to others all or any of the property rights as you see fit. If you retain the full bundle you are said to have *fee-simple title* to the property.

A fee-simple estate (ownership of a particular property) is the broadest, most comprehensive possible type of ownership.

Purpose of Assessment

The assessment of real property has one purpose only—to provide revenue for various local government entities through the property tax. The revenue derived from the property tax provides income for schools, police and fire protection, road maintenance, etc.

The property tax is an ad valorem tax (again, meaning "according to the value" of the property) imposed on all nonexempt land and improvements within the taxing jurisdiction. The income (or lack of income) of the owner has no bearing on the amount of property tax. Chapter 8 describes certain exemptions that take into account the income level of a taxpayer.

Assessed Value

Throughout this book the terms *appraisal* and *assessment* are used. Although very similar, they should be distinguished. An appraisal is an opinion of the value of a property as of a certain date. It may have been arrived at by a professional property appraiser trained in various methods of valuing property. An assessment is a tax assessor's opinion of the value of a property as of a certain date, *and* as recorded on the public tax roll for purposes of property taxation. It is an appraisal of value that takes on additional meaning, in that it is the value officially recognized by the taxing authority. A tax assessor may or may not have the same credentials as a professional property appraiser, but he or she has the authority to decide on the official value, or assessment of a property. In subsequent chapters we will discuss how you may challenge the official assessed value of your property, by offering your own opinion of its value.

Because market and other conditions can change gradually or rapidly, all taxable properties are assessed by the tax assessor as of a certain date, called the *assessment date*. The assessment date provides a snapshot of the various conditions affecting all taxable properties at a specific point in time. This means that if the assessment date is January 1, and you add a new garage on June 5, the assessed value of your home cannot change to reflect the increased value until the following January 1. It also means, using the same assessment date, that if your home burns down on July 5, you will be taxed on the nonexistent home until the next assessment date. While this may not seem fair in certain cases, the alternative is increased confusion in an already chaotic system.

The total assessed value of all the properties within a tax jurisdiction provides the basis for the property tax. The taxation of these properties provides the pool of wealth into which our public officials dip to provide the services they think we need, or the services that we demand.

The Tax Assessor

Tax assessors are responsible for the fairness of all assessments so that a property owner pays no more or no less than a fair share of the property tax. It is the assessor's job to determine the assessed value of all property in the taxing jurisdiction. This assessed value is essentially an opinion that is based on two things: the expertise of the assessor, and the accuracy of all relevant data used by the assessor in valuing a property. In accomplishing the task of assuring tax fairness, or equity, assessors identify, assess, and officially record pertinent information concerning all properties within their jurisdiction.

Assessors are generally well educated professionals. They usually attain their positions through civil service examinations, political appointments, or through the elective process. They are, more often than not, responsive to the taxpaying public. But their responsiveness is tempered by the demand for increased tax dollars from local officials and by the complexity and sheer size of the job which confronts them. It can be a very difficult task.

It is important to realize that tax assessors *do not* set tax rates, nor do they determine the size of the budget. They do not determine where tax money is spent, and, usually, they are not involved in the collection of taxes.

Assessing Real Property

The assessment process is a methodical and rational means of gathering, evaluating, and processing various data in order to arrive at accurate and fair value estimates for real property. It consists of a series of steps that are discussed in the following paragraphs.

The first step—finding and identifying property

The first step in the assessment process is to locate and identify the subject property. This requires a legal description. A *legal description* is one that is recognized by law and that accurately describes a property's boundaries with respect to some point of reference. A street or mailing address is not adequate because it doesn't provide actual physical boundaries. Accepted methods are the government rectangular survey system, the metes and bounds system, and the plat method.

The government rectangular system. The government rectangular system uses north–south lines, called *principal meridians*, and east–west lines, called *base lines*, to locate an initial point within a state. Other north–south lines, called *range lines*, and other east–west lines, called *township lines*, form a grid, or checkerboard pattern, over a state. Each square in the grid contains 6 square miles and is called a *township*. Each township is further divided into 36 sections containing one square mile, or 640 acres. Sections are further divided into quadrants of 160 acres, then sections of 40 acres, 10 acres, and smaller.

The metes and bounds system.   The metes and bounds, or surveyor's method, uses surveying instruments to measure angles and distances from a point of beginning (POB). The beginning point may be a natural or man-made landmark. From the POB, the metes and bounds method provides directions on how to walk to the edge of the property, then walk along the boundaries of the property until arriving back at the POB. It is the most accurate method, and best suited for irregular shaped lots.

The plat system.   The plat system uses a map, called a plat map, that is drawn up by a property developer to describe a proposed subdivision, or by an assessor to reflect changes in an existing neighborhood. The plat map provides an exact description of the subdivision. Each lot is identified by a number and a letter. The dimensions of each lot are also noted. The map generally includes detailed descriptions of streets, sewers, water pipes, and other physical features. Once approved by the appropriate authority, the plat map becomes an official record. It is then assigned an identifying page and placed into a plat book that contains other subdivisions located within or near a particular neighborhood or block. The plat method is the mapping method most often used by assessors.

One of these three mapping methods provide the basis for most assessing department's mapping system.

Assessors commonly use numbers to identify the neighborhoods and individual properties within the taxing jurisdiction. The system used may be similar to the plat system, whereby the assessor assigns each neighborhood or area a number. Individual properties within the neighborhood receive further identifying numbers. For example, 320-13 may indicate lot 13 in neighborhood 320.

The second step—determining the assessment classification

After locating and identifying all taxable property, the assessor determines each property's assessment classification. Property is either real or personal. Both types may be further classified, or described. A property's classification may affect the tax rate which is applied to the property.

Real property is usually further classified by a tax assessor as being residential, commercial, industrial, farm, or vacant. Some tax jurisdictions further divide these primary classifications. An industrial property, for example, may be classified as "light industrial" or "heavy industrial."

States which tax personal property often classify such property by whether it is used in manufacturing or other industrial and commercial uses. Certain types of machinery and equipment may be taxed at one rate, while cars and boats for personal use are taxed at another.

Certain property is exempt completely or partially from taxation. Exempt property may be real or personal property. It may be owned by individuals or by the local, state, or federal government. The extent to which exempt property is excluded from the tax assessing process depends on the local taxing jurisdiction, and will be discussed in greater depth in Chap. 7, "Property Tax Exemptions."

The third step—collecting data

Next, the assessor collects information on which to base the assessment of a particular property. This includes data about the general area, data specific to a property, and data about similar properties.

General data. The subject property is first defined with respect to its neighborhood. This is typically done on the basis of physical, political, and man-made boundaries. What rivers, hills, or wooded areas border the neighborhood? Is the neighborhood in a particular school district, voting district, or township? Do any bridges, railroad tracks, highways, or streets isolate the neighborhood?

After placing a property in a particular neighborhood or area, the assessor looks for information that can physically define the property. What is its location? Is it a good one, or is it near a dump or a stockyard? Is the neighborhood attractive and well maintained, or is it run-down and continuing to deteriorate? Are there sufficient shopping centers, churches, and public means of transportation? The appearance of a neighborhood affects the value of the homes within the area.

What kind of lots are typical of the neighborhood? Are they small or large? Do they have standard or unusual shapes? Is there a flooding problem? Is there an adequate storm-sewer system? What kind of traffic flow is there? Is there heavy traffic? One-way streets or cul-de-sacs?

Are there any potential hazards nearby? Some potentially dangerous neighbors are airports, atomic power plants, and fuel storage facilities.

Is there adequate fire and police protection? Is refuse collected, and are there public parks available? Are there enough schools? Are the zoning regulations adequate to protect the value of homes in the neighborhood? Are building codes up-to-date? Do they require quality building materials? Do building codes ensure that the materials used in the construction of neighborhood homes provide safety features?

Is there any crime? Are children safe from drug dealers? Is there a need for protective measures from burglary? Is the area crowded? Are the people who live there of the same religious and ethnic background?

What trends seem to be at play in the area that could affect property values? Are young families or retired people moving into or out of the area? What are homes selling for? Are there many vacant properties? Are many homes rented? Are any homes being foreclosed? What is the typical income of people in the neighborhood? What type of work is typical of the residents, white or blue collar? What does fire insurance cost?

Specific data. Because land is considered to be permanent, and improvements temporary and subject to deterioration, the assessor needs specific information about both to value them properly. The assessor collects information about the size of the parcel, its shape, the type of soil, and the amount of frontage (the portion bordering a street). He or she also considers nearby improvements like sewers, streets, water hook-ups, etc. Such improvements can increase the value of the land.

The assessor also collects data about any improvements. An *improvement* is any addition to land that increases its value (e.g., a house or a fence.) For a house or condominium, this includes information about its size, style, and age. What is its physical condition? How many rooms does it have? Is there a garage or pool? What is the quality of construction? What about roof type? What is the grade of windows and interior finishing. Are the exterior walls vinyl, aluminum siding, or wood shingles?

Comparative data. The assessor needs comparative cost data on both the land and any improvement to the land. What do similar parcels sell for? What does it cost to build a home like the subject? What have similar homes in the area sold for in the recent past? The assessor will review appropriate records of recent property sales and sources of building cost data to answer these kinds of questions.

Property rights. The assessor must also consider what property rights are involved in the assessment. With single family homes, these property rights are normally the fee-simple title. The *fee-simple title* is the entire bundle of property rights and, typically, the property rights that the average homeowner enjoys.

Private or public restrictions may affect property rights. It is the assessor's task to determine if all the property rights are present. If some are missing, the market value of the home may be affected.

Some examples of private restrictions are easements and deed restrictions. An easement may decrease the value of one property while increasing the value of another. Consider an easement that allows someone to drive a pickup across a residential property to a woodlot. The access increases the value of the woodlot, while decreasing the value of the residential property, because the owner doesn't enjoy full use of the property. A deed restriction may prevent the growing of fruit trees or access to a lake.

Information on private restrictions may be found in deeds or in title reports. Home or condo associations may also place limitations on ownership rights; information on these restrictions may be found in their regulations.

Some public restrictions are building, fire, or electrical codes, and zoning regulations. The codes regulate the types and quantities of building materials, as well as room size and floor plans. They can have a significant effect on value.

Zoning may regulate the size of any improvements, or limit the uses of a property. For example, residential zoning might require certain lot sizes, room sizes, or a certain distance between homes. Or it may prevent you from running a home-based business. Information on zoning and the various public codes may be found in local zoning or planning offices.

These are some of the kinds of data that the assessor collects through interviews, questionnaires, forms, field trips, public records, sales data, etc. The assessor's staff enters the information on property record cards, or other forms of property records.

The fourth step—analyzing the data ————————————————

Once gathered, all of the information must be assembled for the assessment process. Today, it is often entered into computers. Still, this is a huge task. And it is made even more difficult by the fact that it is a continuing process. Everything is always changing, and it is the daunting task of the assessor to attempt to chronicle these changes.

Mass appraisals. Increasingly, the sheer numbers and types of properties have made it impossible, as a practical matter, for the tax assessor and staff to physically inspect every property in their jurisdiction. As a result, some assessors have moved to mass appraisal techniques, which provide a means of valuing extensive numbers of properties at one time, using similar methods and data.

These mass appraisals are generally performed under statutory rules that define the purpose and method of each such appraisal, as well as budgetary restrictions that define its scope and quality. If the statutory basis is not sound and comprehensive, or if economic conditions restrict the scope, the mass appraisal may produce misleading and biased results.

Highest and best use. Once all data is collected, the assessor must determine the highest and best use of the subject property. This is generally considered to be that use which generates the highest net monetary return over a period of time, considering all possible options. Often the present use of a property is its highest and best use. Sometimes, however, an assessor may decide differently.

Consider a house in a residential area that is gradually transforming into a commercial area. While the house provides shelter for its owner, an assessor may determine that the property's highest and best use is as a six story office building, and base the tax assessment on that use. Highest and best use issues may be extremely complex, but fortunately they rarely affect residential properties. If you become involved in a dispute over the highest and best use of your property, you may want to consider seeking professional guidance from an appraiser or lawyer.

The fifth step—determining value ————————————————

After collecting the information, the assessor is ready to determine the market value of the property. This may be difficult because of certain features of real property.

Real property is a one-of-a-kind item. The property your home sits on is the only piece of property exactly like it on the face of the earth. While your lot may look just like your neighbor's lot, it is uniquely different. And while your home may seem outwardly similar to others, yours is unique by virtue of the paint, the carpeting or wooden floors, the way it is lived in, and its exact location.

Real property is immobile. You can't take your land and deliver it to a potential buyer as you can with other commodities. You can't hide it from government taxation or eminent domain proceeding. This immobility also makes your property sensitive to positive or negative conditions beyond your control; an employer may move into or away from your area, or the environment can change for better or worse.

Real property is permanent. Land cannot be destroyed, although improvements such as homes, pools, or barns can deteriorate over time. This aspect generally, but, not always, causes an investment in real property to be of a positive nature.

Three standard approaches for defining the value of real property have developed in response to these characteristics: the market data approach, the cost approach, and the income approach. In applying these methods, the assessor usually follows guidelines contained in an assessment manual issued at the state level. This manual provides instructions for telling when and how to use each of the three approaches.

There are many types of "value" in the world of real estate. The assessor in your state will likely use a statutory definition of market value. Be sure to find out from the assessor what that definition is. It will probably be similar to the following definition:

> *Market value* is an estimate of the price that a property would likely bring if offered for sale on the open market by a knowledgeable, willing seller to a knowledgeable, willing buyer.

This definition assumes that:

1. Market value applies to a certain date and may change with the passing of time.
2. The terms of the sale are for cash or its equivalent.
3. The property is offered for sale for a reasonable time period.
4. The seller and buyer are both fully informed about the property.
5. The seller and buyer are under no coercive pressure to conclude a sale.
6. The seller can deliver a clear title.

With this definition of market value in mind, let's briefly consider the main ways in which a tax assessor values property.

The market data approach. The basis of the market data approach is that the actions of buyers and sellers in the market place actually show what real world buyers and sellers are willing to spend and surrender their property for.

With the market data approach, also known as the comparable sales approach, the assessor determines the market value of the subject property by comparing it with similar properties sold recently in the same area. It follows the premise that the market will establish a price for the subject property in the same way that the market set the prices of comparable properties. It is particularly important because it makes use of the actual responses of buyers and sellers to the market. It is probably the most reliable and convincing approach for valuing homes.

The market data approach is also favored with mass appraisals. Various statistical methods provide the means to analyze data gathered from the marketplace.

The cost approach. The basis of the cost approach is that an informed buyer would pay no more for an improved property than the cost to build a similar improvement on land of comparable value.

With the cost method, the assessor first estimates the value of the land as if it was vacant. Then the assessor estimates the cost to reproduce or replace the improvement based on local construction costs on the assessment date. Next, the assessor deducts any accrued depreciation on the improvement. Finally, the assessor adds the value of the land to the depreciated cost of the improvement.

The cost method may yield a higher valuation than the market data approach. Tax assessors like it for this reason, and because it lends itself to mass appraisals. It works best with new construction, and is likely to give an inaccurate value indication for older structures.

For mass appraisals, the assessor organizes accurate and up-to-date information on the prices of construction materials from cost manuals. This data is applied to large numbers of properties in a uniform fashion. The assessor will also use the market data method to determine market value for broad classes of properties. The data from both methods is combined to arrive at the mass appraisal value conclusions.

The income approach. The basis of the income approach to value is a mathematical relationship between the amount of net income a property can be expected to produce annually, and a capitalization rate derived for the property. This approach is primarily used with income-producing property. Because the income approach can be complex, and because essential information may not be available or pertinent to residential properties, it is not commonly used to value houses or condominiums. It is beyond the scope of this book, and it is not used by a residential taxpayer challenging a high property-tax assessment.

The sixth step—correlating the results

Certain approaches are more appropriate for particular types of properties. The market data approach provides no help in the valuation of a racetrack, an aquarium, or any property where little or no comparative sales information is available. The cost approach is not relevant to the valuation of a vacant lot. And, because most homeowners buy their homes for shelter and not to produce an income, the income approach is usually inappropriate for assessing residential properties.

The assessor may use any or all approaches in determining assessment value. For residential properties, the most relevant approaches are the market data and cost approaches. And, because each approach examines different aspects of market value, the results are usually not the same. They may be fairly similar, or quite different.

After obtaining indications of value from these approaches, the assessor reaches the next step in the valuation process. This step involves correlating the results to produce one final indication of value—the assessment. Because each approach uses different data, simply averaging the results does not produce the final result. Instead, the assessor has to consider several factors.

How much data has been collected for each approach? Is the data reliable? Is it accurate and up-to-date? Which approach has been used in this neighborhood before, and with what results? Is this a new neighborhood where the cost approach can be used? Or is this an older neighborhood with enough recent comparable sales to effectively use the market data approach?

After considering these kinds of factors, the assessor decides a final opinion of value and the assessment is done.

Appraisal reports. At the conclusion of the assessment process, the results of the assessor's appraisal are recorded in an appraisal report. The purpose of the appraisal report is to provide persuasive proof of the assessor's opinion of value.

There are two kinds of appraisal reports: the form appraisal and the narrative appraisal. Both types may be simple or complex. They are designed to record all of the relevant information about a particular property, and to support a particular value judgement.

Because of the many appraisals that an assessor must perform, the form appraisal is the type he or she will normally use. A property record card is the usual basis for an assessor's form appraisal. This is a record that you will want to review for your own property.

Later in this book you will see how mistakes can creep into property record cards, resulting in erroneous tax bills. You will also see how a professionally prepared appraisal report, if available to you, may be used to review the assessor's property record card.

The seventh step—preparation and certification of the tax role

When the initial appraisal process is complete, the assessor has to prepare and certify the assessment role. To do this, the assessor makes a public announcement stating that the initial assessment and valuation data for all real property in the taxing jurisdiction is ready and available for public inspection. The instrument for this public announcement is often the local newspaper.

At this time, taxpayers may examine this information, and if there is a dispute, present any opposing evidence. If the arguments are valid, the assessor may change the initial assessment, and the incorrect data, informally.

After the initial assessment, the assessor files the tentative assessment roll (used for taxing purposes) and again announces publicly:

That the tentative assessment roll has been filed.

When and where it is available for public review.

When and where the local board of assessment review will meet to consider formal complaints.

At this time, taxpayers may, again, examine the tentative assessment role. However, in most jurisdictions, the assessor may not legally change an assessment after the tentative roll has been recorded. If there is a disagreement, the only remedy is through a formal complaint to the local board of assessment review.

The local board of assessment review. The local board of assessment review (the name varies depending on location) consists of a number of individuals who are knowledgeable about local property values. They are usually appointed by a local government entity. The purpose of the board is to decide assessment appeals in a fair and impartial manner.

The local board of assessment review begins its annual meeting after the tentative roll has been filed. The meetings of the local board are open to the public, and normally last until all complaints have been heard. The local board of assessment review is empowered to hear complaints, to decide cases between the assessor and the taxpayer, and to change assessments after the tentative roll date. Any complaint not filed by the end of the local board's meeting will not be heard until the following year.

After the local board's session, the assessor files the final assessment roll used for taxing purposes. At this time, the assessor is required to announce that the final assessment roll has been filed, and when and where it is available for review.

The assessor then provides the taxing authority with the final assessment roll, and the total assessed valuation of all taxable property. The taxing authority uses this information to compute the tax rate, and to send out tax bills.

Determining the tax rate. Each fiscal year, local government taxing units—counties, cities, school districts, towns, and villages—prepare an operating budget. This budget is an estimated cost of operating every aspect of that local unit's activities for the coming fiscal year.

After determining its operating budget, the taxing unit estimates its revenue from all other sources (such as court fines, parking tickets, licenses, and sales taxes). The taxing unit decreases its operating budget by these amounts; what remains is the amount of money that it needs from property taxes to satisfy its individual operating budget.

The taxing unit receives the final assessment roll, containing the total assessed value of all taxable property (our earlier pool of wealth) from the assessor.

The taxing unit needs to get a certain percentage of the total assessed valuation to satisfy its operating budget. This percentage is the *tax rate.*

The taxing unit determines the tax rate by dividing the budget by the total assessed value. The resulting tax rate is then multiplied by each property's assessed value in order to produce each individual tax bill.

Consider a county where the total assessed value of properties on the tax role is $900,000,000. The county's budget is $20,000,000, and it has revenue from sources other than property taxes of $4,000,000.

$$\$20,000,000 - \$4,000,000 = \$16,000,000$$

It still needs $16,000,000 from property taxes to meet its budget obligations.

To determine the tax rate, the remaining budget obligation is divided by the total assessed valuation:

$$\$16,000,000 \div \qquad \$900,000,000 \qquad = \quad 0.018$$

$$\text{(budget)} \quad \div \quad \text{(total assessed value)} \quad = \quad \text{tax rate}$$

The rounded result (0.018) is the percentage of the total assessed valuation required to satisfy the budget obligations. Multiplying each property's assessed value by the tax rate (0.018), and then adding all the results, yields the needed $16,000,000.

The tax on a home assessed at $100,000 at this rate is now:

$$(\$100,000 \times 0.018) = \$1,800$$

The tax rate depends on the amount of the budget and the total assessed value. If the budget increases while the total assessed value stays the same, the tax rate goes up. For example:

$$\$18,000,000 \div \$900,000,000 = 0.020$$

The tax is now:

$$(\$100,000 \times 0.20) = \$2,000$$

If the budget decreases while the total assessed value stays the same, the tax rate goes down:

$$\$14,000,000 \div \$900,000,000 = 0.015$$

The tax is now:

$$(\$100,000 \times 0.015) = \$1,555$$

If the budget stays the same while the total assessed value goes up, the tax rate goes down.

$$\$16,000,000 \div \$980,000,000 = 0.016$$

The tax is now:

$$(\$100,000 \times 0.016) = \$1,600$$

Expressing the tax rate. The tax rate is normally expressed in dollars per $100 of assessed value, or in dollars per $1,000 of assessed value (known as mills).

Mills are thousandths of a dollar, or 1/10 of a cent. To find the tax on a home assessed at $100,000, with a tax rate of 16 mills per dollar, proceed as follows:

1. Convert the mills to a tax rate by dividing the 16 mills by 1,000:

$$(16 \div 1,000 = 0.016)$$

2. Multiply the assessed value by the converted tax rate:
$$(\$100{,}000 \times 0.016) = \$1{,}600$$

To find the tax on a home assessed at $130,000, with a tax rate of $1.50 per $100, proceed as follows:

1. Divide the assessed value by $100.
$$(\$130{,}000 \div \$100 = \$1{,}300)$$
2. Multiply the result by the tax rate.
$$(\$1{,}300 \times \$1.50 = \$1{,}950)$$

To find the tax on a home assessed at $90,000 with a tax rate of $15 per thousand, proceed as follows:

1. Divide the assessed value by $1,000.
$$(\$90{,}000 \div \$1{,}000 = \$90)$$
2. Multiply the result by the tax rate.
$$(\$90 \times \$15 = \$1{,}350)$$

Assessed Value versus Fair Market Value

So far, we have discussed value in terms of fair market value. We have said that fair market value is the actual cash value that would be paid by a willing buyer to a willing seller, or what common sense tells us the property is "worth."

Not all assessors actually assess property at fair market value. Many tax jurisdictions use some percentage of fair market value other than 100 percent. For example, all property may be assessed at a statutorily defined rate of 40 percent of fair market value. In this case, a home with a fair market value of $100,000 would have an assessed value of $40,000.

Many homeowners are relieved to see that their home is valued by the assessor at less than what they know to be its fair market value. In many cases, however, the assessment may actually be based on more than the fair market value, but, because only a percentage of market value is reflected on the tax bill, the homeowner is satisfied with the assessment.

As an example, your tax bill indicates your property is valued by the assessor at $97,500. You know it would sell for $120,000 on the open market, and, therefore, conclude you are getting a great deal. However, since the assessor is basing the assessment on 65 percent of fair market value, he or she really has overvalued your home considerably, as shown:

$$\text{Fair market value} = \$120{,}000$$
$$\text{Assessed value} = \$97{,}500$$

Dividing the assessed value by 0.65 reveals the assessor actually considers the fair market value to be $150,000:

$$\$97,500 \div 0.65 = \$150,000$$

The property should be assessed at 65 percent of $120,000, or $78,000, rather than $97,500.

Summary

This chapter has examined the valuation process from the assessor's point of view. The major points of this chapter are:

1. The purpose of the assessment process is to provide the basis for the property tax.
2. The tax assessor is responsible for the fairness of all assessments.
3. The assessment process is a logical and methodical process that arrives at accurate and fair estimates of property value by:
   a. Locating and identifying property.
   b. Classifying property by type.
   c. Collecting relevant data.
   d. Analyzing data.
   e. Determining value, using the three approaches to value.
   f. Correlating the results.
   g. Preparing and certifying the results.
4. The tax rate is derived from the total assessed value of a taxing jurisdiction and its required operating budget.
5. Assessors may value a property at fair market value, or at some fraction of fair market value.

Grounds for Challenging
Your Property Tax Assessment

Life is unfair.

MILTON FRIEDMAN (b. 1912),
American economist

Property taxes, like life, are unfair. When they are unfair it is because they have violated the principle of tax equity. Tax equity requires that property be valued accurately to begin with, and, once valued, that it be taxed at the same rate as other properties in its class. There are only three primary reasons why a property-tax assessment may be inequitable:

1. The assessment contains *mechanical errors.*
2. The assessment contains *valuation errors.*
3. The assessment contains *legal errors.*

In this chapter, we will explore all three grounds for challenging an unfair assessment.

As we consider these types of property assessment errors, remember that an assessment may contain any or all of them. Certain kinds of assessment mistakes may belong in more than one category at a time.

Mechanical Errors

Mechanical errors are mistakes in description and measurement of the property, or record keeping errors of some kind. These kinds of errors will be the easiest for you to spot, since you know your property better than the assessor does. They are often obvious mistakes that the assessor overlooks for one reason or another. Because of this, they are the kind of assessing mistakes that an assessor will most readily correct if pointed out.

Measurement errors

The two measurement errors most likely to be made by the assessor are (1) incorrect land size and (2) incorrect building gross square foot size measurements.

Land measurement errors. Land measurement errors occur for various reasons. If your property is square or rectangular, or made up of several regularly shaped sections, it is a fairly easy matter for someone to calculate the total square foot or acreage size. However, if your land has a highly irregular shape, the likelihood of measurement errors becomes far greater. It is possible, too, that parts of neighboring parcels have been included in the total size of your land. This can occur because the assessor depends upon out-of-date records of property sales, or improperly drawn plat maps. Surprisingly, many people really don't have an accurate idea of the size of their own property.

It is always a good idea to review the deed to your property to determine exactly how much land you own. Compare this with the assessor's records. Depending upon the age of the deed, and the way it describes your land, you should be able to determine, with fairly good accuracy, just how big your property is. Some older deeds are not as precise in this respect as more modern ones. They may describe the boundaries of your land in terms of features that no longer exist, such as "Bob Smith's fence to the west, and the large oak tree to the north."

If the property deed is not helpful in determining the size of your land, consider measuring it yourself. For smaller lots this is an easy matter. If you have reason to believe the assessor's record of land size is greatly in error, it may be worth it to have your land professionally surveyed. This is especially true regarding large, irregular lots, whose size may only have been estimated long ago.

Home measurement errors. Errors in the measurement of your house or condominium also occur for various reasons. Possibly the assessor never actually measured your home, but "guestimated" its size based on seemingly similar neighboring homes. Perhaps your condominium unit was mistakenly recorded as one of the larger style units in your development. Or, maybe you applied for a building permit for an addition on your home, but later changed your mind and never built it. The building inspector forwarded the permit to the assessor who, presuming the addition was built, increased the size of your home in the property records.

Just as with irregularly shaped land, more complicated house designs invite measurement errors. If for example your home is a highly unusual modern design, containing various living levels and odd angles, it is more likely to have been measured incorrectly than would be a home of a more simple design.

Measure your home yourself to verify the accuracy of the assessor's records. Measure along the exterior walls. Draw a sketch of the perimeter of the house, labeling the length of each side. If your house is a simple rectangle, multiply width times length to derive its gross area in ft^2. If the house has multiple stories, add the gross square footage of all the stories together to derive the total. If your house contains more than one basic rectangular section, record the area of each smaller section and then total them, as in Fig. 3.1.

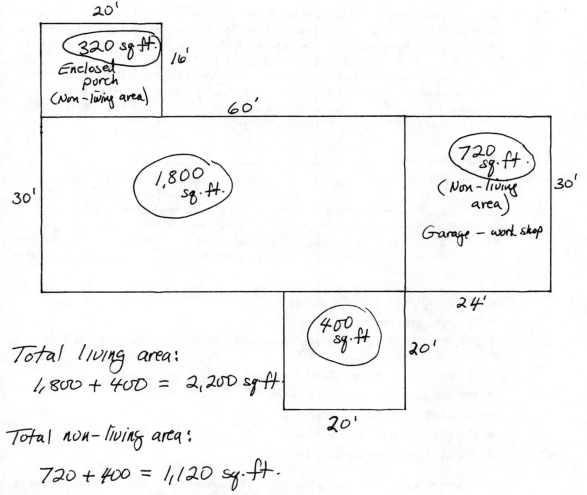

Figure 3.1. A typical floor plan sketch showing living space.

Finally, be sure to separate living areas from nonliving areas when measuring your home. Nonliving areas such as garages, patios, decks, and screened in porches are valued at lower rates by the assessor, than are living areas of the home. If the assessor's total square foot measurements for your home are considerably more than your own measurements, it is possible that nonliving areas were inadvertently included.

Copying or mathematical errors

After measurement errors, the next most likely mechanical errors are those involving copying or mathematical mistakes. There are many opportunities for assessors and their staffs to record erroneous property information. Property record cards, plat maps, sales ratio studies, building permit records, and deed records may, in total, contain hundreds of data entries for each property in a tax district. With every entry there is a chance for human error. Once recorded, such mistakes may not be corrected for many years.

Although the math used by assessors in most kinds of property records is simple addition, subtraction, multiplication, and division, mistakes occur frequently. Chapter 5, "The Cost Approach" contains a detailed example of how to check for math errors found in a typical property record card.

Descriptive errors

Lastly, errors in the description of a property may cause it to be valued incorrectly. These errors may be obvious, or very subtle. A detached garage may be listed in the assessor's records when, in fact, it was razed several years earlier. A house may be described as having four bedrooms and two fireplaces when in fact it has three bedrooms and one fireplace. The condition of the home may be described as very good when it is really only fair. Other kinds of descriptive errors may involve the following:

- The number of stories in a home
- The type and quality of construction
- The kinds of special features (fireplaces, alarm systems, sprinkler systems, custom interiors etc.)
- The amount of depreciation accrued
- The condition of the neighborhood
- The kinds of utilities available
- The desirability of the location
- The quality of the landscaping

The number of different ways in which assessors may describe properties is almost unlimited. When you review your own property records, look for anything at all that is inconsistent with what you know to be true about your property. While not all descriptive errors result in incorrect appraisals of value, the likelihood of the assessed value being in error increases with each such mistake.

Adverse factors omitted from property description. There is another type of descriptive error that can occur, which we will call an error of omission. It may be that when you study the property records for your property, everything appears to be correct. However, there may be factors not reflected in the records which, if brought to the attention of the assessor, could result in a lower value assessment.

These kinds of adverse factors may be inside or outside of your home. For example, there may be a serious accumulation of radon gas in your basement, or a recently discovered toxic waste dump in the neighborhood. Your home's foundation may have extensive cracks, or perhaps you found out that large amounts of asbestos were used in building your home, which now must be properly removed in order to make certain repairs to the house. Your home might be extensively damaged by termites, or suffer from periodic flood damage.

Any of these kinds of problems could prove expensive to remedy, and you should bring them to the attention of the assessor. Be certain, however, that they have not already been accounted for by the assessor. For instance, if the existence of the toxic waste dump was known about for many years, its affect on the value of your home has probably already been considered, even if it was not specifically described by the assessor on your property record card.

The following are some other examples of the kinds of adverse factors that may have been omitted from consideration when the assessor valued your home.

Factors external to your property

- A housing surplus
- High unemployment
- Unfavorable zoning changes
- Lack of services or amenities, such as trash collection, sidewalks or street lights
- Environmental problems such as poor air or water quality
- Natural problems such as inadequate water supplies or heavy wind or water erosion

Factors internal to your property

- Aluminum wiring
- Poorly designed floor plan
- Inadequate insulation
- Lack of storage areas
- Antiquated plumbing and heating systems
- Major structural defects
- Substandard landscaping
- Lack of easy access to utilities

Valuation Errors

Valuation errors are those caused by incorrect application of one or more approaches to value, resulting in an incorrect assessed value for a property. Recall that one of the primary functions of a tax assessor is to render an official opinion of value—the assessment—for all properties in a jurisdiction. To be fair and equitable, assessments must be accurate, and they must be fair *in relation to other properties in the same class.*

Satisfying these requirements is a several-step process. The assessor first develops an opinion of the fair market value of a property, based on one or more of the major approaches to value (primarily the cost and comparable sales approaches for residential properties).

Any number of problems along the way can result in valuation errors. The assessor may utilize the approaches to value incorrectly. He or she may rely upon data that is out of date, inaccurate, or insufficient. Mistakes made anywhere in the valuation process can result in valuation errors. Understanding the basic working of these approaches, therefore, will help you determine whether or not valuation errors have occurred.

After deciding on an opinion of value for the property, the assessor converts the fair market value to an assessed value if the tax jurisdiction uses an assessment ratio less than 100%. For example, if the assessment ratio is 50%, a property with a fair market value of $100,000 would now have an assessed value of $50,000. If the assessor has valued your home at more than fair market value to begin with, the assessed value (either 100 percent of fair market value or some lesser percentage) will be in error.

Once completed, the assessment must withstand a final test. It must be fair in relation to assessments on similar properties in the same class. The final step in the assessment process, therefore, is to compare the assessment against assessments of similar properties.

If most other homes are assessed at only 40% of fair market value, the home in our example would be over assessed. Its $50,000 assessed value is $10,000 higher than it should be. This is not an uncommon situation. Frequently properties are assessed at more or less than the "official" assessment ratios.

Equalization studies and sales assessment ratio studies

There are two specific tools which assessors use to gauge the fairness of an assessment, in relation to both the officially mandated assessment ratio and the actual assessment ratio. They are known as equalization studies and sales assessment ratio studies. If they are used in the tax district where your property is located, you should be able to review copies of them in the assessor's office, or write to the state or county assessing departments to find out how you may gain access to them. The following is a brief description of each.

Equalization studies. *Equalization studies* are usually done by state or county assessing officials. Their purpose is to compare the assessment of properties within all the tax districts in the state or county. Depending on which state you live in, each tax district within your state or county may tax properties at different rates, and at different percentages of fair market value. The equalization study allows "apples and oranges" to be compared by converting the various tax rates and assessment ratios to a common denominator. You can then more easily compare the assessment on your home with assessments on the overall class of residential properties in your state or county.

Some state or county level assessing departments use equalization studies as a means of auditing the accuracy of lower level assessing departments which they oversee.

Not all states utilize equalization studies. If yours does, you can use it as a tool to help decide on the fairness of your home's assessment.

Sales assessment ratio studies. *Sales assessment ratio studies* are comparisons of the actual selling prices of a class of property with the assessed value for the class. These studies are usually done at the state or county level, and sometimes by individual assessing offices.

In a typical sales assessment ratio study, a representative number of property sales in a tax district are selected. The assessed value of each of the properties is divided by its sales price. The resulting figure, expressed as a percentage, represents the sales assessment ratio. The ratio for all of the properties in the study are then averaged.

The average sales assessment ratio for the class of properties may then be used to compare with the ratio of assessment on your own property. If your property assessment differs significantly from the average sales assessment ratio for other residential properties, the assessment is likely in error.

Equalization studies and sales assessment ratio studies are not necessarily useable as proof that your assessment is in error. They may, however, help support your contention of an overassessment, when used with other evidence.

Neither of these studies can be used to discover specific errors made by the assessor in valuing your property. However, once you know the fair market value of your home, they can help indicate if its assessed value is fair, in relation to the assessed value of other homes.

Ask yourself the following questions to help determine the fairness of your property assessment and whether or not valuation errors have occurred:

- Is your property assessed at more than fair market value, or more than the allowable percentage of fair market value as mandated by law?
- Is your property assessed more highly than similar properties in your neighborhood?
- Is your property assessed the same as more valuable properties in the area?
- Is your property assessed more highly than the same class of residential properties in your area, as demonstrated by an equalization study?
- Is your property assessed at a greater percentage of fair market value than other properties in its class, regardless of the state mandated assessment ratio, as demonstrated in a sales ratio study?

Answering yes to these kinds of questions suggests the possibility that valuation errors have been made in the assessment of your property.

Legal Errors

The final category of assessment errors are *legal errors*. These are assessment errors which violate some aspect of local, state or federal law. Legal errors may also be valuation errors, or they may be errors which have nothing to do with the actual appraisal of your property's value.

Since each state's laws regarding property assessment and taxation vary, it is not possible to list all the ways in which legal errors may occur. However, the following are typical for many states.

- Property was assessed for more than fair market value, or for more than the percentage of fair market value allowed by law for the particular class of property.
- The percentage of assessed value increase was greater than the amount allowed by law in the revaluation period.
- The property was included in the wrong class of properties (i.e., commercial rather than residential).
- The property was listed as being in the wrong tax district, either completely or partially.
- The assessor did not allow exemptions to the assessment, which the property owner was entitled to and had properly applied for.
- The assessor did not use the approach or approaches to value mandated by law, or ignored data that would have resulted in a different opinion of assessed value.
- The assessor did not follow other procedures, as specified in the state approved assessing manual.
- The assessor ignored, or disregarded statutory or case law, regarding specific assessing doctrine in his or her tax district.
- The assessor did not actually visit the property to perform an appraisal as required by law.
- The assessor did not certify the tax roll by giving official notice of its completion, or failed to follow other procedures prescribed by law in validating the tax roll.
- The assessor did not give official notice of the new assessment to the owner.
- The revaluation of properties in the tax district did not adhere to mandated mass appraisal techniques, or was not performed by a qualified person or persons, as described by law.
- The owner listed on property records is not the owner of the property.
- Personal property was incorrectly identified as real property, or vice versa.
- Property was not assessed as of the official assessment date.
- Assessor did not take into account unusual restrictions to property rights assessed, either of a governmental nature such as zoning or health and safety codes, or of a private nature such as easements and rights-of-way.

■ The assessor or staff was grossly negligent in carrying out the duties of his or her office.

State laws describe, in exacting detail, how property should be valued and how property taxes must be administered. Some sources of up-to-date information regarding the laws in your state include:

■ State assessing manuals
■ Other publications available through state, county, or local assessing departments
■ Published state statutes, available in municipal libraries as well as university or law school libraries

State assessing manuals are often the best source of information concerning what constitutes legal assessing errors in a particular state. They offer specific guidance for assessors (and taxpayers as well), in interpreting the ever changing statutes and court decisions that affect the assessor's day-to-day duties.

Summary

This chapter has examined the three major grounds for challenging a property-tax assessment:

1. The assessment contains mechanical errors.
2. The assessment contains valuation errors.
3. The assessment contains legal errors.

Mechanical errors are mistakes in description or measurement of a property, or record keeping errors of some kind. Description errors may or may not result in an inaccurate opinion of value.
Valuation errors are those resulting in an incorrect opinion of value. They occur when the cost or comparable sales approaches to value are utilized improperly, resulting in an incorrect value. They may also result when properties are not assessed fairly in relation to similar properties.
Legal errors are assessment errors which are in violation of a local, state or federal law.
Some assessing errors may fall into more than one category at a time.
Equalization studies and sales assessment ratio studies are tools used by assessing offices to help gauge the accuracy and fairness of assessing practices.

The Assessor's Office and Beyond

Public officers are the servants and agents of the people, to execute the laws that the people have made.
GROVER CLEVELAND

What to Expect

Cleveland's statement contains words to keep in mind as you enter the assessor's office. Remember, assessors and their staffs are there to serve the public. That means you.

There are many thousands of taxing districts in this country, each with its own assessing office. Each operating in a state with its own unique tax laws and assessing regulations. These offices share many similarities, but differ in the quality and size of the assessing staff, procedures and methods of operation, helpfulness to the public, and the number of properties they are charged with assessing each year.

There is the office located down in the basement of the 50-year-old town hall. It is dark with boxes piled high behind a high wooden counter that you approach for information. There seems to be no one around. The dark wood of the counter gleams from all the elbows that have rubbed it over the years. That noise down on the floor behind the record stacks may be a mouse, or worse.

Or you may walk into the future. This office is large and the lighting is bright. Numerous computers sit on large, high tables waiting for your fingers on the keyboard. Behind a low formica counter, a number of smiling, friendly clerks ask you how they can help. There are forms and booklets available to explain how everything works.

Depending upon the style of local government in your area, you will be visiting a village, town, city, or county assessor's office. Each assessor's office performs the same basic functions.

Remember that most of the assessor's staff know what they are doing. They see people come in each and every day asking the same basic questions. Questions that are probably answered in the pamphlet or letter that accompanied the tax bill.

They see belligerent and angry people... confused and struggling people... vocal and intelligent people... people with one purpose: to make sense out of the system and get some relief.

But they rarely see people who understand the purpose of the assessor's office. Who understand what the process is and how it works.

This is not surprising. The assessing process is complex and confusing. Always was and always will be.

But because the average tax payer sometimes has no idea what is going on, it makes it very difficult for the clerks to help. Can you imagine a clerk taking the time to explain all of the subjects covered in this book? It's no wonder that it's often difficult to get information from the assessor's office.

Just as the actual offices are physically different, so is the way that information is provided to the public.

In some offices it is very difficult to get any kind of information. While this often seems a definite policy, more often it's just that no one has taken the time to set up a clear and understandable routine to handle or help the public. There is so much other work and so few staff, that available resources are put where it seems they'll do the most good.

At the other end of the spectrum, there is the office that makes every effort possible to accommodate the public. All kinds of data are made available, including information about the appeal process.

In between are the vast majority of offices that provide some relevant data and instructional material. That try to help as best they can.

The type of office you walk into is the luck of the draw. Much depends on the assessor who runs that office.

Assessor Qualifications

Few assessors start out in life with the goal of becoming an assessor. Often they are college-educated people who pass a civil service test or win an election. Typically, assessors are well educated and experienced professionals, the majority of whom belong to professional organizations like the International Association of Assessing Officers (IAAO). The IAAO limits its regular membership to elected or appointed assessment officials. (Other types of memberships are available.)

The IAAO and other similar organizations help assessors by keeping them up to date on issues that are of special concern. They accomplish this through seminars and training courses, as well as books, newsletters, and videos about subjects like computerized appraisals, urban appraisals, appeal procedures, and mapping techniques.

Each state has different qualifications for becoming an assessor. Some require specific academic degrees or backgrounds. Other states require no special educational experience, but expect that assessors pass certain college level or professional courses within a probationary time period. Still other states have no requirements other than passing a civil service test or winning an election. In some areas, assessors are political appointees.

You may be worried that your assessor doesn't have solid qualifications. This is a legitimate concern, but one that is becoming more and more unlikely as time goes by.

Increasingly, states are requiring that assessors meet exacting certification standards. To accomplish this, states are providing training and assistance to even the smallest taxing jurisdiction. This training focuses on appraisal principles, mass appraisal techniques, and administrative questions.

How the Assessor's Office Functions

The assessor is charged with determining the assessed value of all taxable property within the local taxing jurisdiction. This is quite a task. The next time you're driving through your town or city, consider that the assessor is responsible for valuing almost every building, house, and property that you see. To help, states have developed assessing manuals.

Assessing Manual

The State Department of Revenue (or whatever department supervises tax collection in your state) prepares a manual of instructions for all assessors and other officials who are involved with the property-tax system. The manual provides directions for handling most of the situations that may arise in the assessment process.

The assessing manual contains just about everything an assessor would need to know about the property-tax system, including exemptions, mapping requirements, how to use the income, cost, and market approaches to arrive at market value, how to handle appeals, what factors to consider in deriving just valuation, the duties of the assessor, how to inspect properties, essential forms, as well as important tax court rulings and interpretations. It's the assessor's bible and it explains the assessing process in more detail than any of us would ever want or need to know.

It is available to the public for a nominal cost in many states. If you inquire about purchasing one, you may be told that they are not in stock, or being updated. Be persistent. Follow up until you receive a copy.

It is up to the individual assessor to follow these guidelines. Most assessors do; others may prefer to go their own way, referring to the assessment manual only when they come across some unique problem.

Information Available

Each assessing office ordinarily decides how much information to make accessible to the public. Some offices provide a great deal, while others are sparing in what they make available. Of course, it's up to each assessor to follow any state guidelines.

Most assessors realize that the public doesn't understand the assessment process. They may try to help by printing pamphlets or booklets that explain how to appeal an assessment in a general way.

It is not necessarily their job to describe a very complex process in enough detail for the average homeowner to successfully appeal an assessment. That would be quite a task. But they also know that there has to be some kind of pressure relief valve for the taxpayer.

So what happens is that some pieces of this very complicated puzzle are offered to the public. Not enough to help everyone who might be enraged momentarily by a property-tax bill, but enough to get the really persistent ones started down the right path.

Some of this information and its uses are explained in the following paragraphs.

Tax maps

Assessor's offices have tax maps that are available for public perusal. They may be plat maps, aerial maps, or neighborhood maps. (See Chap. 2 for a description of typical mapping systems used by assessors.) They show the exact dimensions of parcels, and can be used to identify the dimensions of your property and any comparable properties you have selected.

Tax maps are contained in very large books that show every lot or parcel in a taxing jurisdiction. You can locate the tax map for your neighborhood by looking in one of several (depending on the size of the taxing jurisdiction) larger maps, called index maps, or in manuals that lists all the neighborhoods and subdivisions within a taxing jurisdiction.

Your neighborhood (or the neighborhoods of any comparable properties you're interested in) will be identified so that you know what tax map book contains your property.

If you have any trouble, ask for help.

Tax roll

The tax roll can provide you with information about comparable properties. It identifies all taxable properties by owner and by the property's parcel identification number for a given tax year. It provides the property's legal address, property type, the assessed value, and taxes paid or due.

The tax roll may be in a number of huge manuals, or it may be computerized. It changes from one year to the next, so be sure you look in the right tax roll.

List of local taxing jurisdictions

The list of local taxing jurisdictions shows you where your tax money is going. It lists each local governmental unit that gets a share of your property-tax money. If you are claiming an exemption, you'll want to find out which local jurisdictions, if any, allow the exemption.

List of property sales

Assessors maintain extensive records of all property sales within their jurisdictions. They have many uses for this information, including market data approaches to value. This information is usually made available to someone contesting an assessment. After all, it's entirely within your rights to know which comparable properties the assessor used in determining your assessment.

Property record card

This is a very important piece of your appeal puzzle. It is the record where the assessor enters all the information about your home to determine your assessment. Most assessor's offices will make this available to you. Others will provide only an abbreviated version.

You want to see your property record card and the property record cards on any comparable homes that you select. In some jurisdictions, these cards are not readily available, and you may, at first, be denied access to the property record cards for comparable properties. However, it is our position that these are public records that may rightly be reviewed by all interested citizens. There is absolutely no justification for an assessing office to make these records secret and unavailable to you the taxpayer. Be persistent about your right to see them.

A property record card may be completely filled in or it may contain very little information. It can be smudged, torn, and years out of date. Or it may be a computer generated form that is updated yearly. It may have coded entry fields; you will have to ask what the fields mean.

The following paragraphs reference Fig. 4.1, a typical property record card. Be aware that property record cards come in all types and conditions. The information in the sample is typical.

1. *Identification* provides the parcel ID number, the legal address, and information about the owner. The owner may live at a different address than the property's address.
2. *Record of ownership* shows who owned the property, when they took possession, and the sales price. This can be useful in verifying the sales prices of recently sold comparable properties. Other information refers to property class and use. The book and page numbers refer to the officially recorded property deed, usually located in a bound volume in the county registry of deeds, or local courthouse.
3. *Assessment record* shows the assessment history over a period of time. For each assessment, the land and house are valued separately and then combined together for a total value.

    Visits by the assessor's staff are noted. If your property was not actually visited during a revaluation, its value will be estimated. Obviously there is more chance of error occurring in the assessment if a visit has not been made.

Parcel #: 032-232-000	RECORD OF OWNERSHIP	DATE	BOOK	PAGE	PRICE	Class	RES
56 Henning Drive	Heinrich, Hans H. etal	10-12-79	2911	248	117,500	Zoning	R1
OWNER: Ronald & Elisa Smith 56 Henning Drive Anywhere, NH	Nelson, Thomas etal	2-15-85	3719	110	195,000	Use	SFR
	Smith, Ronald + Elisa	6-19-90	4114	307	215,000	NH Code	RES

INSPECTION WITNESSED BY:

ASSESSMENT RECORD

	1979	1983	1988	1992	19	19	19	Visit History
Building	43,000	51,600	90,300	93,075				J.R. 3-11-79
Garage/Non-living	4,500	5,400	9,450	8,942				L.D 5-1-88
Other								L.D 4-1-90
TOTAL VALUE BUILDING	47,500	57,000	99,750	102,017				L.O. 5-1-91
TOTAL VALUE LAND	53,000	63,600	111,300	120,000				
TOTAL LAND & BUILDING	100,500	120,600	211,050	222,017				

LAND VALUE COMPUTATIONS AND SUMMARY

Description	Code	Size	Rate	Influence Factor	Land Value
Primary site	01	30,000	2.00	+5%	63,000
Secondary site	02	1.0 ac	57,000		57,000
Undeveloped					
Marshland					
Waterfront					
TOTALS					120,000

Property Factors		
TOPOGRAPHY		STREET
Level ✓		Paved ✓
Hilly		Sidewalk ✓
Swampy		Unpaved
NEIGHBORHOOD		IMPROVEMENTS
Improving ✓		Water ✓
Static		Electric ✓
Declining		Sewer ✓

NOTES: Applied for building permit to add extension on home on 9-12-91. No construction begun yet.

Figure 4.1a. Property record card (front).

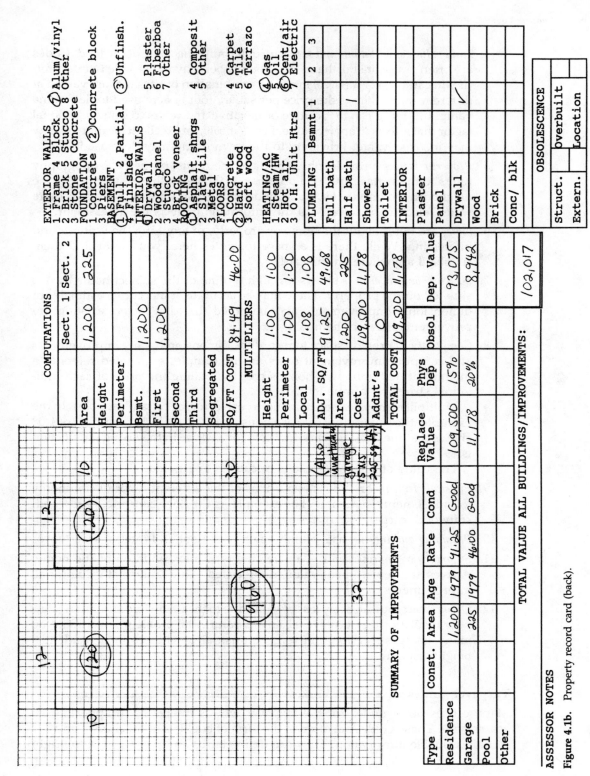

SUMMARY OF IMPROVEMENTS

ASSESSOR NOTES

Figure 4.1b. Property record card (back).

4. *Land value computations and summary* determine the value of the land. Codes are often assessor shorthand that you may or may not be able to interpret. (If you can't, ask.) A parcel may be a combination of sites that are valued at different rates. Rate is the price per square foot or acre used to determine value. Influence can be positive or negative and refers to some additional factor that affects property value. For example, an excellent location or view may increase value. Proximity to the town dump may decrease it.

5. *Property factors* provide physical data about the property. Topography refers to the surface area of a property. Is it level, hilly, or swampy? Is the neighborhood improving, static, or declining? How are the streets? Is there water, electric, or sewer? All this information affects the assessment.

6. *Notes* are notes about the home or property, or anything the writer found interesting. While there is a space for notes here, you might find them scribbled anywhere on the card.

7. *Sketch of improvements* shows a rough outline of the subject home as it is situated on the property. There may be accurate or inaccurate estimates of dimensions. Improvements may be noted that don't exist; existing improvements may not be noted.

8. *Computations* provide space to record the dimensions of any improvements and compute improvement costs. In the sample, segregated refers to a method of determining a home's cost by totaling the price of each individual structural component.

   Multipliers may be used to adjust a cost factor for certain variables. In the example, the square-foot cost of a house is $84.49. A local multiplier of 1.08 shows that the actual square-foot cost for a house in the taxing jurisdiction is $91.25.

   The value of each structure is calculated and noted.

9. *Physical elements* are brief descriptions of the different types of commonly found elements in a home. For example, is the floor concrete, hardwood, softwood, carpet, tile, or terrazzo?

10. *Plumbing and interior* lists plumbing on each floor and interior wall types.

11. *Summary of improvements* evaluates the type and condition of the home. Arrives at a replacement value, depreciated value, and total value for all improvements.

12. *Obsolescence* indicates any loss of value due to the following: structural (e.g., poor insulation), external (e.g., an environmental problem), overbuilt (too many garages), or location (e.g., industrial businesses in a residential neighborhood).

Taxpayer guides

Many offices have guides for the taxpayer who is interested in appealing an assessment. These guides are often in the form of booklets or brochures, and can contain valuable information. They can define terms and point you in the right direction for an appeal. Try to get all the information that your assessor offers.

Perhaps the most important information available in the assessor's office concerns local procedures. What forms are necessary for an appeal, and what are the important dates of the property-tax calendar?

Forms are very important. Even more important is that you fill out forms correctly and completely. If you don't, your appeal may be disallowed for insufficient data.

Ask what forms are necessary. Get extra copies and look at them carefully making sure that you understand what is required in each section. If you aren't absolutely certain, ask for help. It is essential that you fill out forms completely and accurately.

Ask for a copy of the tax calendar. The tax calendar contains all the important dates of the tax year including the assessment date, the notification date, the tentative assessment-roll filing date, assessment appeal deadline, tax payments due date, and the local board of assessment review meeting dates.

While they are customarily fixed dates, any one of them may be changed from one year to the next. If they are and you don't know about it, you lose. Be sure to check tax calendar dates each year.

Some offices allow time extensions to gather data. Check to see if they are available in your area.

State or county equalization studies and sales assessment ratio studies

In Chap. 3 we discussed how you can use equalization studies and sales assessment ratio studies to support your opinion of overassessment. Both may be useful in helping you determine the fairness of your own property-tax assessment.

If your assessor does not maintain either of these types of studies for your use, ask where you may locate copies. If they have been undertaken in your area, the assessor can likely tell you where to find them. He or she can also tell you if they are useable as proof of an unfair tax assessment. If not useable as proof, they may still be useful to support your other evidence of an overassessment.

Cost manual

What cost manual does the assessor's office use? Is it a standard commercial manual or an in-house manual that the assessor's staff has compiled? This information will be important when reviewing the assessor's cost approach to the value of your home.

Although these manuals are not usually made available to taxpayers, you should be able to arrange an appointment to review this manual. This will be important, especially if you have reason to suspect that the assessor's cost valuation of your property is in error.

If you perform a cost valuation of your property using a commercial cost manual, you may want to see how the assessor's version differs from your own. The best time to do so may be at an informal meeting with the assessor. This can be an excellent opportunity for you to see exactly how the assessor's cost manual was used in valuing your property.

Other Information

The assessor's office keeps records of ownership changes, building and property characteristics, individuals and properties eligible for exemptions, trends in market prices, construction costs, and typical leases to estimate the value of all assessable properties.

The following is a list of the type of information that an assessor's office generally needs to function smoothly and correctly. The information may or not be available to the public. Check with your assessor to find out.

If your assessor does not provide this type of data, look to other sources (e.g., planning agencies, libraries, colleges, builders, code enforcement agencies, and commercial real estate offices).

1. Permits to build, demolish, repair, or renovate property (generally filed by neighborhood or subdivision). This information usually originates in the building inspector's office and is forwarded to the assessor's office since it affects property value.

2. Sales and rental data for neighborhoods or subdivision (provides the basis for the assessor's valuations). Detailed lease information about specific properties may not be available to you since this is often confidential in nature. However, lease information will generally not be part of your residential tax appeal. If you need such information for other reasons, the assessor can provide information on typical lease terms in your area.

3. Current construction costs (data about new cost factors that is normally updated quarterly).

4. Building codes, fire codes, zoning requirements. Depending upon the organization of your local government, this kind of information may also be found in a planning department or building inspector's office.

5. Housing market trends.

6. Operating costs for certain types of commercial and industrial property.

7. Current trends in development and building.

8. Proposed subdivisions.

9. Proposed utility installations.

10. Proposed street improvements.

11. Traffic patterns and volumes.

12. Community planning and development.

13. Population density and characteristics of neighborhoods.

Beyond the Assessor's Office

Tax bill

You can find a copy of the latest tax bill for each property in the tax collector's office. You'll most likely find it in manual form or in a computer. Figure 4.2 shows a typical tax bill. The following paragraphs refer to the numbered sections in the figure.

1. *Tax year:* The fiscal tax year may differ from the calendar year. Be sure that your tax appeal is for the same tax year as indicated on the current bill.

2. *Tax due date:* If you are appealing your tax assessment, you still have to pay your tax bill on time. If you win, you will get money back. If you don't pay your bill on time, you will end up paying interest on the amount due, and you risk having a lien placed on your property if you delay payment for a long period.

3. *Tax rate:* This shows the tax rate for residential, commercial, industrial, and vacant property. You can see how different property types are taxed at different rates. Each local taxing jurisdiction (town, county, schools, and sewers) taxes at a certain rate per thousand, or per hundred dollars. The combined rates are the total tax rate for each property class. In the example, for residential property, the tax per thousand dollars for the town, county, schools, and sewer add up to $12.44 per thousand dollars.

4. *Property identification:* Shown here is the parcel identification number, the tax bill number, and the legal address. Each is important and should be used in any correspondence with the assessor's office to positively identify your property.

5. *Taxpayer identification:* This is the name of the owner(s).

6. *Exemptions:* These are the exemptions that apply to the property, and that have been granted to the owner.

7. *Land value:* This value is always assessed separately from improvements.

8. *Building value:* The assessed values of any improvements (like a house) to the land.

9. *Total value:* The assessed values of the land and improvements are added together to give the total assessed value.

10. *Total tax:* The residential tax rate is $12.44 per $1,000. To determine the total tax, multiply $221,355 by 0.01244. The result is $2,753.65.

11. *Total exemptions:* The total value of the exemptions granted to the taxpayer.

12. *Total payment due:* The total tax ($2,753.65), minus total exemptions ($250), equals the total payment due ($2,503.65).

1992 REAL PROPERTY TAX BILL
TOWN OF ANYWHERE, NH 00234

Office of the Collector of Taxes
123 Main Street
Town Hall
Anywhere, NH

OFFICE HOURS:
9:00 TO 5:00
MON. to FRI.

Tax payable at collector's office
or by mail. Include SELF ADDRESSED
STAMPED ENVELOPE for receipt if
desired.

TAX DUE DATE: OCTOBER 15

TAX RATE PER $1000	RESID.	COMM.	INDUST.	VACANT	PROPERTY IDENTIFICATION	TAXPAYER IDENTIFICATION	EXEMPTIONS	
Town	$5.45	$7.75	$7.75	$1.87	PARCEL #: 032-232-000	Ronald & Elisa Smith	03 VETERAN	$150
County	$0.85	$0.85	$0.85	$0.85	TAX BILL #: 3467	56 Henning Drive	07 BLIND	$100
Schools	$4.93	$4.93	$4.93	$4.93	LOCATION:	Anywhere, NH 00234		
Sewer	$1.21	$2.22	$2.22	$1.21	56 Henning Drive			
TOTAL	$12.44	$15.75	$15.75	$8.86				

LAND VALUE	BUILDING VALUE	TOTAL VALUE	TOTAL TAX	TOTAL EXEMPTIONS	TOTAL PAYMENT DUE
$120,000	$101,355	$221,355	$2,753.65	$250.00	$2,503.65

TAXES ARE DUE IN FULL ON DUE DATE.   UNPAID TAXES ARE SUBJECT TO 12% INTEREST AFTER DUE DATE

Figure 4.2. Tax bill.

Professional appraisal reports ————————————————————————

Often, all the information about your property can be found on the property record card. The assessor bases the assessment of your property on the information that the property record card contains.

However, you may already have in your possession a more detailed description of your property in the form of an appraisal report. An *appraisal report* is the document prepared by a professional appraiser when valuing your house.

If you received such a report for a mortgage application or some other reason, you may use it to compare with the assessor's valuation of your home. It may contain a good basis for finding errors in the assessor's records of your home's value, especially if it is recent. A professionally prepared appraisal report will almost always be more detailed and complete than the assessor's own records.

The appraisal report provides actual evidence of the assessment in a logical and intelligible manner. It may be a form appraisal or a narrative appraisal.

The form appraisal is generally done on a specific form that is devised to record applicable data in a way that leads to, and supports the assessment. An appraiser may use an in-house form or any of several commonly used appraisal forms.

The narrative appraisal is often a multipaged document that guides the reader through the assessment process in extensive detail. It provides the necessary data to support the assessment in a very convincing way.

A narrative appraisal normally contains the following or similar sections:

1. A *letter of transmittal* identifies the subject property, gives the effective date of the appraisal, the value conclusion as of that date, and identifies the appraiser. The rest of the report supports the value conclusion.

2. The *purpose of the appraisal* defines why the appraisal is being done. Most often, it's to determine the market value of the subject property. Market value is defined and the property is further identified.

3. *Factual data* provides regional, city, town, and neighborhood data. It may refer to population, local government type, available transportation, public facilities and services, recreational and medical facilities, or any other pertinent data. Maps and photographs may be shown.

4. The *property description* provides a detailed description of the land and improvements. Describes the dimensions of the land with text and maps. Describes any improvements with text, illustrations, photographs, or drawings.

5. *Assessment, taxes, zoning* typically gives data about the most recent assessment and property taxes paid. Present and possible future zoning is given. Also information about how the property can legally be used.

6. *The highest and best use* defines highest and best use and then offers an opinion of the highest and best use of the subject property.

7. *Market value, analysis and reconciliation* defines the three approaches (market data, cost, and income) to value. Then shows, in detail, how each approach

yields its value determination. Reconciles the values attained with each approach and arrives at an expert opinion of the property's value.

8. *Qualifications* provide the credentials of the appraiser.

Summary

This chapter describes the assessor's office and the type of information that a taxpayer can find there. It also describes other important kinds of information such as appraisal reports.

Assessors are typically well-educated, experienced professionals. Each state sets the qualifications for its assessors. States also provide assessment manuals that provide guidelines for assessors to follow.

An assessor's office generally provides tax maps, the tax roll, a list of local taxing jurisdictions, a list of property sales, property record cards, and taxpayer guides.

Information about cost manuals, sales assessment ratio studies, and equalization studies may or may not be available.

Other information that can be helpful consists of appraisal reports and tax bills.

The Cost Approach

Nowadays people know the price of
everything and the value of nothing.
OSCAR WILDE (1854–1900),
Anglo-Irish author

Wilde might have been thinking of the problems facing the tax assessor who must find often elusive values for not just one or two, but many thousands of properties. Compared with a private practice appraiser who is afforded the luxury of time when appraising an individual property (and who charges several hundreds of dollars to do so), the often harried town or city assessor is faced with a very different challenge. Although he or she may carry the same professional appraisal credentials as a private appraiser, the fact remains that all the properties within the tax district must be periodically revalued within certain time constraints. State statutes prescribe how often a tax district must perform these revaluations.

The solution to the problem increasingly has been the use of mass appraisal techniques. The method of choice for assessors practicing mass appraisals is most often the cost approach. They may support the mass appraisal results with the comparable sales approach. But the cost approach is the primary vehicle used in mass appraisals. Even in tax districts where a heavy workload is not a hindrance to the accurate and timely revaluation of residential properties, the cost approach is the one most often relied upon by assessors.

In this chapter we will examine the cost approach in greater depth. We will look at ways to spot the errors that are an inevitable by-product of mass appraisals. Then we will show how to gather the information you need to perform a cost valuation of your home so that you can check your property assessment. Understanding how a tax assessor uses the cost approach to value your home can be invaluable to you when challenging your assessment.

The Cost Approach

The cost approach arrives at a value determination by estimating the cost to reproduce or replace a building based on current local construction costs, deducting from the new construction costs accrued depreciation on the existing structure, and then adding the estimated land value to arrive at a total cost.

The reasoning behind the cost approach is simple. A knowledgeable buyer would not pay more for a given property than the amount required to purchase similar land, upon which could be built improvements (e.g., a home, barn, or other permanent structure built on the land) identical to, or of comparable utility to, the property in question. In other words, a property is only worth what it would cost to replace it with a similar property.

Therefore, when using the cost approach to value a property, we are faced with two distinct problems. The land must be valued as if empty, and the cost of replacing or reproducing the improvements on the land must be calculated. *Reproduction cost* refers to the expense of building an exact duplicate of the improvements, whereas *replacement cost* refers to the cost of constructing improvements of similar utility, but not of the exact dimensions and style. Replacement cost is often used in lieu of reproduction cost, since the expense of making an exact replica of an older building may be much more than merely constructing a building of similar utility using modern building techniques. In some cases, it may be next to impossible to duplicate an older building due to unusual design features that are no longer reproducible. Whether replacement or reproduction cost is chosen as the basis of a cost valuation of a property, it must be used consistently throughout the process, and not interchanged with the other.

When an appraiser uses the cost approach to value a home or other property, he or she will do the following:

1. Value the land as if it was not improved (had no house, paved driveway, etc.) and as if it could be used for its highest and best use.

2. Estimate the costs involved in reproducing or replacing the existing improvements to the land. The types of costs considered will include direct costs such as labor and materials, indirect costs such as architectural and engineering fees, and profit costs, that reflect the amount of profit a developer could expect to make developing and selling such a property.

3. Calculate the amount of accrued depreciation to the value of the existing improvements and subtract this amount from the current replacement or reproduction cost. Depreciation (as discussed in the next section) can result from a number of causes including physical wear and tear on the property, and the obsolescence of certain features of the property.

4. Combine the value of the land, as if vacant and used for its highest and best use, with the depreciated value of the property improvements. The combined value is the value of the total property using the cost approach.

Depreciation and obsolescence

Depreciation of a property improvement may occur for numerous reasons. Perhaps the most common kind of depreciation is that caused by the physical deterioration of the building or other improvement due to age. Very few buildings are made to last through the centuries, and most have a far shorter life span. Roofs need replacement, paint fades and peels, floors wear out, and plumbing leaks.

Another sort of depreciation of value occurs for reasons outside of physical wear and tear. "Obsolescence" can cause a property's value to drop even though the building involved may be in very good condition. For example, an older office building, in a prime downtown location, may be worth less than newer competing buildings, because of outdated floor plans and a lack of conveniences such as high speed elevators and central air conditioning. This is known as *functional obosolescence. External obsolescence* refers to factors external to a property that cause it to lose value. An example of this is a factory which is outmoded due to a completely new, and less expensive, modern method of manufacturing that replaces the old method.

Finally, physical deterioration and obsolescence is either "curable" or "incurable." A leaking roof is an example of a *curable* deficiency that can easily be fixed and will usually contribute some positive value to the building. Other kinds of defects cost far more to fix than they are worth and are considered *incurable.* For example, a poorly designed floor plan in an older home may cost more to change than it would ever contribute in value to the renovated home.

Consider, for a moment, some potential pitfalls awaiting those who trust blindly in the accuracy of the cost approach. The approach depends on the use of reliable and current local construction costs in the value equation. Depreciation must be calculated precisely. The value of the land, as if vacant and available for its highest and best use, must also be derived in some reliable fashion. The potential for inaccuracy is large, especially if some, or all, of the needed data is not available or completely accurate. The effect of each erroneous bit of data is magnified in the final value conclusion. Older buildings, in particular, become difficult to value using this method.

Professional real estate appraisers are well aware of the limitations of the cost approach. The problems are not insurmountable, and when the cost approach is applied carefully, high degrees of accuracy may be obtained. An appraiser will use multiple methods of valuing properties when possible, so that a final value conclusion may be derived.

In a perfect world, all three methods, the cost, market data, and income methods, would result in the same concluded value, but often they will differ. When this occurs, the professional appraiser uses his or her best judgement, relying upon the method or methods for which the most and best data was available.

For someone wishing to challenge an overly high tax assessment, checking the accuracy of all the assumptions in a cost valuation may lead to a successful argument for lower taxes.

Ways of Estimating Cost When Using the Cost Approach

The several steps required to perform a cost valuation of a property described so far are simple enough. It would be logical to wonder at this point however, just how are the costs of a home or other building estimated? Where do you get the kind of accurate and detailed cost data that will result in a valid cost estimate for a property? More to the point, where does the tax assessor get the information that helps determine the value of your property and, thus, the size of your tax bill? There are several usual ways in which this information is derived.

Cost manuals

The most common source of construction cost data for residential properties is a *cost manual*. While there are different ways of organizing the cost data within these manuals, the most usual for residential property use is known as the *comparative unit* method. Using a database of historical building costs, the cost for construction of a particular type of building is broken down into some common unit, such as a square foot, cubic yard, or square meter. For instance, the cost of building a home in a particular area may be $60 per square foot. Multiplying the square foot area of a home by this figure would give the cost new for construction of the home (not including land value). Property tax assessors will most often rely upon some version of the comparative unit method of estimating construction costs when using the cost approach.

A tax assessor may establish and maintain an in-house database of building costs for the local area, or may depend upon commercial cost-estimating services for such data. Several well-known companies maintain extensive national databases of building cost data and offer access to them through subscription services. These companies include F. W. Dodge Corporation, Marshall & Swift Publication Company, and Boeckh Publications. When checking the accuracy of a property's assessed value for tax purposes, it will be useful for you to know how the cost data was derived, and if it fairly reflects the cost of construction as of the tax assessment date.

The *segregated cost* method of estimating construction costs depends upon a far more detailed summary of the costs of individual building components. The quantity and cost of each component of a building, such as the heating and air conditioning units, roof shingles, linear feet of foundation material, fireplace, chimney and brickwork, etc. are totaled to arrive at a new construction cost for the entire structure. Labor costs are also included in the individual component costs.

Another cost-estimating method is known as the *quantity survey* method, which is an even more detailed breakdown of all the individual expense items that go into construction of a building. This method would typically be used by a contractor concerned with exactly estimating the cost of a project. It is not a method that a tax assessor would likely use for valuing a residential property, because of the amount of time and effort required. For the same reasons, someone preparing a challenge to a tax assessment would not usually rely upon it either. However, in the case of a newly constructed home, where such detailed cost information may be available to the homeowner, the actual construction costs may be useful in challenging the assessor's estimated construction cost.

Depreciation and cost multipliers _____

The cost approach requires that depreciation of a building be accounted for. Land is never depreciated. A tax assessor arrives at the depreciated value of a building in several ways. A physical inspection of the property may be performed, from which the tax assessor may conclude physical deterioration and obsolescence values. The assessor may use commercially available cost-estimating manuals which include depreciation tables for various classes and ages of buildings. Lastly, an assessor may use his or her own depreciation schedules, compiled using property data from the local area.

In addition to depreciation tables, cost manuals usually include some kind of *multipliers* or *factors*, which are used to adjust the base square-foot construction costs for local variables. For instance, a base square foot cost of $61.50 may be listed as the average construction cost of a home in a certain region of the country. Within the geographical region, multipliers may be applied to the base figure to account for cost differences within sections of the same region. Multipliers may raise or lower the base cost. A multiplier of 1.05 applied to the base cost ($61.50 × 1.05) results in a higher base cost of $64.57/ft^2 for a particular area. There are various kinds of multipliers used in cost manuals. Later in this chapter, we will see how multipliers are used by tax assessors in a property record card example, and in a commercial cost manual example.

To avoid the expense of purchasing one of the commercial cost manuals for a yearly review of your property assessment, you may be able to locate a copy in the local library. Other sources include real estate agents and property appraisers who may be willing to lend their manuals. Find out if the tax assessor uses an assessing manual, or maintains an in-house database of local building costs to perform cost-approach valuations. These public documents and records may be available for your use.

Cost approach example _____

The following is an example, in summary form, showing the major steps involved in a cost-approach valuation of a property. It uses the comparative unit method of computing building value. For this illustration, we will presume the comparative unit cost data is supplied from a commercial cost service manual, and that land value has been obtained by review of comparable land sales.

The subject property is a 10-year-old, 1950 ft^2, single story, ranch-style home with vinyl siding, poured concrete foundation, and full, unfinished basement. It is located in a well kept neighborhood and is built on a 25,000 ft^2 lot, similar in size to many other neighborhood lots. The home is in good condition.

Step 1: Site valuation. Review of several sales of good comparable home sites in the neighborhood indicates that similar land is currently valued at $1.09/ft^2. Thus the value of the subject site is:

$$(\$1.09 \times 25{,}000 \text{ ft}^2) \text{ or } \$27{,}250$$

Step 2: Determination of replacement cost. The commercial cost manual indicates that current construction costs for ranch style homes in the same region of the country average $56.50/ft². The cost to construct a replacement of the subject home, presuming no adjustments must be made to the base square-foot cost, is therefore:

$$(\$56.50 \times 1{,}950 \text{ ft}^2) \text{ or } \$110{,}175$$

Step 3: Determination of accrued depreciation on home. Depreciation tables, found in the commercial cost manual, show that a 10-year-old ranch-style home, in good condition would be expected to depreciate in value by 9 percent. Said another way, the house would retain 91 percent of its value, compared with a new home. Applying this depreciation amount to the replacement cost new derived in Step 2, the depreciated value of the home is found to be:

$$(\$110{,}175 \times 0.91) \text{ or } \$100{,}259$$

Step 4: Combine land and depreciated building values. The current total value of the subject home is equal to site value plus depreciated building value, or:

Site value:	$ 27,250
Depreciated building value:	+ $100,259
Current total value:	$127,509

Rounded off, the subject property is valued at $127,500.

Commercial Cost Manual Example

Figures 5.1 and 5.2 are front and back examples of a completed cost valuation of a home using the commercially available Marshall & Swift square-foot cost method. Many assessing offices utilize Marshall & Swift cost data in performing residential property assessments. Even if the assessor in your area does not, it will help you to review these forms, since they illustrate the factors an assessor accounts for when using the cost approach. The following is a general description of the forms, explaining how the final value for the property was derived. All cost entries in the forms are derived from the current Marshall & Swift *Residential Cost Handbook*. The appropriate pages are reproduced in Figs. 5.3 through 5.7.

Property description

The property being valued is a single family, single story, 12-year-old ranch. It is located near Atlanta, Georgia, and has an attached garage and screened in porch. It has wood-shingle siding, an unfinished basement, and is fully carpeted throughout.

With that simple description, let's look at how the "Square-Foot Appraisal Form" (Figs. 5.1 and 5.2) is completed.

SQUARE FOOT APPRAISAL FORM
For use with the RESIDENTIAL COST HANDBOOK

Appraisal for __Sample__   Property owner _____

Address __Atlanta, GA__

Appraiser _____   Date _____

TYPE		QUALITY		STYLE		EXTERIOR WALLS		GARAGE TYPE	
Single Family	☒	Low	☐	No. Stories	1	Hardboard/Plywood	☐	Detached	☐
Multiple	☐	Fair	☐	Bi-level	☐	Stucco	☐	Attached	☒
Town House	☐	Average	☐	Split Level	☐	Siding or Shingle	☒	Built-In	☐
Row House	☐	Good	☒	1½ story - Fin.	☐	Masonry Veneer	☐	Subterranean	☐
Manufactured		Very Good	☐	1½ story - Unf.	☐	Common Brick	☐	Carport	☐
House	☐	Excellent	☐	2½ story - Fin.	☐	Face Brick or Stone	☐	Garage Area	

FLOOR AREA | BASEMENT AREA: Unf. __1300__ ; 2½ story - Unf. ☐ ; Concrete Block ☐ ; __209 sq. ft.__

1st __1300__   Fin. _____   End Row ☐   MANUFACTURED   BALCONY AREA

2nd _____   NUMBER OF PLUMBING   Inside Row ☐   Alum., Ribbed ☐   _____

3rd _____   Fixtures __6__   NUMBER OF MULTIPLE   Lap Siding ☐   PORCH BRZWY. AREA

Total_____   Rough-in __1__   UNITS _____   Hardboard ☐   (a) __300 sq. ft.__

Plywood ☐   (b) _____

		Quan.	Cost	Extension		
1.	COMPUTE RESIDENCE BASIC COST: Floor area x selected sq. ft. cost	1300	52.10			67730
2.	SQUARE FOOT ADJUSTMENTS:			+	−	
3.	Roofing					
4.	Subfloor					
5.	Floor Cover _carpet through out_	1300	2.91	+		3783
6.	Plaster Interior					
7.	Heating/Cooling _heat pump_	1300	1.37	+		1781
8.	Energy Adjustment _mild climate_	1300	1.01		−	(1313)
9.	Foundation _mild climate_	1300	1.24		−	(1612)
10.	LUMP SUM ADJUSTMENTS:					
11.	Plumbing	3	950		−	(2850)
12.	Fireplaces _single, one story_	1	2625	+		2625
13.	Built-in Appliances _allowance_	1	3225	+		3225
14.	Miscellaneous (Dormers)					
15.	SUBTOTAL ADJ. RESIDENCE COST: Line 1 plus or minus Lines 2-14					73369
16.	BASEMENT, UNFINISHED	1,300	10.87	+		14131
17.	Add for basement interior finish					
18.	Add for basement outside entrance					
19.	Add for basement garage: Single ☐ Double ☐					
20.	PORCH/BREEZEWAY, describe _screened, open slab_	300	6.99	+		2097
21.						
22.	SUBTOTAL RESIDENCE COST: Total of Lines 15-21					89597
23.	GARAGE OR CARPORT - sq. ft. area x selected sq. ft. cost	209	23.80	+		4974
24.	Miscellaneous (roofing adjustment)					
25.	SUBTOTAL GARAGE COST: Line 23 plus or minus Line 24					4974
26.	SUBTOTAL OF ALL BUILDING IMPROVEMENTS: Sum of Lines 22 and 25					94571
27.	Current Cost Multiplier _1.00_ x Local Multiplier _.96_			X		.96
28.	REPLACEMENT COST NEW: Line 26 x 27					90788
29.	Depreciation: Age _12_ Condition _good_ Deduction _11_ % of Line 28					9987
30.	Depreciated cost of building improvements: Line 28 less Line 29					80801
31.	Yard improvements cost: List, total, apply local multiplier and depreciate on reverse side					
32.	Landscaping cost: List and compute on reverse side					
33.	Lot or land value					35000
34.	**TOTAL INDICATED VALUE:** Total of Lines 30-33					115801

FORM 1007   *See back of page for sketch and computations*

Figure 5.1. Appraisal form.

Explanation of completed form ——————————————————

Note, at the top of the form (Fig. 5.1) that basic items such as type, quality, and style are checked as appropriate. Items that are not checked do not apply to the property. Each of these entries will affect the base square-foot cost of the home, as derived from the cost manual.

The total square-foot floor area, basement area, and porch/breezeway area are entered, as computed from the sketch on the reverse side of the form (Fig. 5.2).

Continuing down the form, each item that is appropriate to the property is entered. Any lines that are left blank do not pertain to the sample property.

Line 1: The basic square-foot cost, taken from the cost manual, is multiplied by the area of the residence. The result, $67,730, is entered on this line.

Lines 2–9: Square-foot adjustments to the base cost are made, to account for items which are better or worse than the average for this style and class of building. The first adjustment made is item 5, "Floor Cover." Since the house is fully carpeted, an additional amount of $2.91/\text{ft}^2$ is added to the base cost. Likewise, a positive adjustment is made for the home's heat pump, which is of higher cost than the standard for this type of property. Negative adjustments are made for items 8 and 9, "Energy Adjustment" and "Foundation."

Lines 10–14: Lump-sum adjustments are additional features that are not considered in the average base cost of this type of property. The cost of one fireplace and built-in appliances, typical for this type of home, are added here.

Line 15: The subtotal cost of the residence, considering all positive and negative adjustments to value, is entered here.

Lines 16–19: The cost of the basement is computed and entered here.

Lines 20–21: The cost of the screened-in porch is computed and entered here.

Line 22: The subtotal cost, including the residence, basement, and porch, is entered here.

Lines 23–25: The cost of the garage is entered here.

Line 26: The subtotal of all building improvements, including the garage, is entered here.

Line 27: Current cost multipliers and local multipliers are taken from the manual and combined here. These multipliers, applied to the subtotal of building costs on line 26, will account for variables in local labor and material costs.

Line 28: Replacement cost new for this home, not accounting for depreciation.

Lines 28–30: Depreciation is calculated from depreciation charts in the manual and applied to the amount on line 28. The depreciated cost of the improvements is entered on line 30.

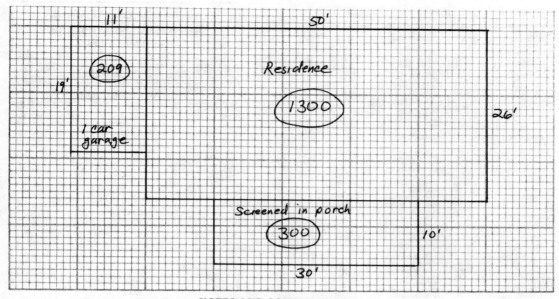

NOTES AND COMPUTATIONS

Area computations:

Residence   50' X 26' = 1300 sq. ft.
Garage   11' X 19' = 209 sq. ft.

Rear screened in porch   10' X 30' = 300 sq. ft.

Figure 5.2. Sketch and computations acccompanying the appraisal form.

Lines 31–33: Land-value calculations are made here. In the example, no adjustments have been made to the lot value of $35,000.

Line 34: Total indicated value of property, including depreciation of the improvements and total land value.

Valuing Land When Using the Cost Approach

Land must be valued separately from improvements on the land when using the cost approach. How is the value of land derived? The primary method is by analyzing the sales prices of similar parcels of land. Although there are other methods which can be used, this is the most common one, and also the one most likely to be used by a tax assessor. When valuing land, an appraiser or tax assessor will consider the land as if vacant and available for its highest and best use, even though a home or other improvement exists on it.

ONE STORY

Square Foot Costs
Good Quality

RESIDENCE:

	WOOD FRAME				MASONRY		
Total Area	Stucco	Siding or Shingle	Masonry Veneer	Total Area	Common Brick	Face Brick or Stone	Concrete Block
800	$56.27	$56.52	$62.71	800	$63.31	$71.56	$59.23
1000	54.19	54.43	60.07	1000	60.66	68.33	56.95
1200	52.55	52.78	58.00	1200	58.57	65.80	55.15
1400	51.20	51.42	56.30	1400	56.87	63.73	53.67
1600	50.06	50.28	54.88	1600	55.43	61.99	52.43
1800	49.07	49.29	53.65	1800	54.19	60.50	51.35
2000	48.21	48.42	52.57	2000	53.11	59.19	50.41
2400	46.75	46.95	50.76	2400	51.28	57.00	48.81
2800	45.55	45.75	49.27	2800	49.79	55.21	47.51
3200	44.53	44.73	48.02	3200	48.53	53.71	46.40
3600	43.66	43.85	46.95	3600	47.45	52.41	45.45

SQUARE FOOT ADJUSTMENTS:

ROOFING:
Wood shingle	(base)
Comp. shingle/built-up rock	− $ .95
Wood shake	+ .14
Clay tile	+ 3.32
Concrete tile	+ 1.17
Metal, formed seams	+ 2.19

SUBFLOOR:
Wood subfloor	(base)
Concrete slab	− $2.06

FLOOR COVER:
Allowance (if not itemized)	+ $3.62
Resilient floor cover	+ 3.19
Carpet	+ 2.91
Wood Flooring	+ 8.09
Ceramic tile	+ 7.72
PLASTER INTERIOR:	+ $2.26

LUMP SUM ADJUSTMENTS:

PLUMBING: 11 fixtures + rough-in (base)
Per fixture	+ or − $950
Rough-in	+ or − 285

FIREPLACES:
Single, 1 story	$2,300 - $2,950
Double, 1 story	3,175 - 4,550

HEATING/COOLING:
Forced air	(base)
Oil-fired	+ $ .40
Electric, radiant	− .11
Baseboard or panel	− .14
Hot water, baseboard	+ 1.02
Radiant	+ 1.18
Warm & cooled air	+ 1.20
Heat pump	+ 1.37
Air-air exchange sys.	+ .86

ENERGY ADJ.: Moderate climate (base)
Mild climate	− $1.01
Extreme climate	+ 1.81
Superinsulated	+ 3.15

FOUNDATION: Moderate climate (base)
Mild climate	− $1.24
Extreme climate	+ 1.52

BUILT-IN APPLIANCES:
Allowance (if not itemized)	+ $3,225
Range & Oven	+ 1,460
Hood & Fan	+ 285
Dishwasher	+ 575
Garbage Disposer	+ 215
Trash Compactor	+ 465
Exhaust Fan or Bath Heater	+ 130
Radio Intercom	+ 775

BASEMENT: Outside entrance: $1,230

Unfinished basement:	200	400	800	1200	1600	2000	2400
Concrete walls	$23.25	$16.25	$12.77	$11.11	$10.15	$ 9.60	$ 9.08
Concrete block walls	20.63	14.54	11.36	9.95	9.27	8.75	8.36
Add for finish, minimal	6.02	5.25	4.58	4.23	4.00	3.82	3.69
partitioned	24.80	21.84	19.06	17.62	16.71	16.17	15.66

PORCH/BREEZEWAY:

	Floor Structure:			Wall Enclosure:			Add For Roof	Add For Ceiling
Area	Open Slab	Open W/Steps	Wood Deck	Screen Only	Knee Wall W/Glass	Solid Wall		
25	$ 4.28	$11.06	$16.59	$12.60	$41.88	$28.49	$10.32	$ 2.92
50	3.91	9.66	14.33	8.40	27.92	18.99	9.52	2.76
100	3.73	8.62	10.37	6.30	20.94	14.24	8.97	2.58
300	3.49	6.83	7.02	3.50	11.63	7.91	8.04	2.34

GARAGE:

	Area	Stucco	Siding or Shingle	Masonry Veneer	Common Brick	Face Brick or Stone	Concrete Block	Add For Finish
Attached	200	$23.57	$23.80	$25.83	$28.40	$32.13	$24.67	$ 3.80
	400	17.61	17.65	18.61	19.74	20.57	18.17	3.16
	600	15.29	15.33	15.84	16.61	16.94	15.49	2.89
Detached	200	$28.71	$28.88	$32.04	$36.32	$40.36	$30.10	$ 4.45
	400	21.90	21.87	24.08	26.71	29.22	23.08	3.58
	600	19.47	19.93	21.35	23.50	25.19	20.48	3.29

Basement Garages, add lump sum to unfin. bsmt. costs: Single: $1,165, Double: $1,635
Carports: Shed or Flat roof: $8.38, Gable roof: $11.89

Figure 5.3. One-story appraisal factors (Courtesy Marshall & Swift, Residential Cost Handbook, © 1991 Marshall & Swift).

Residential Cost Handbook
QUARTERLY MULTIPLIERS
SEPTEMBER 1991

The Current Cost and Local Multipliers should be used to trend the costs published on the preceding pages to a current date and to adjust the costs by location. This section is republished quarterly and is based on averages of two Marshall & Swift Building Cost Indexes from three districts as published in the Marshall Valuation Service. Other conditional adjustments are found on page F-9. Comparative Cost Multipliers for residential construction are on page F-10.

CURRENT COST MULTIPLIERS

Use the following Current Cost Multipliers by district (see map below) to trend the costs on the preceding cost pages to a current level.

PAGES	EASTERN		CENTRAL		WESTERN	
	FRAME	MASONRY	FRAME	MASONRY	FRAME	MASONRY
SECTION A						
A-1 to A-92 (Single Family, Detached)	1.00	1.01	.98	.98	1.00	1.01
A-93 to A-116 (Mobile/Mfg. Housing)	1.02	1.02	.99	1.00	1.02	1.01
A-117 to A-134 (Multiple Residences)	1.01	1.01	.98	1.00	1.01	1.02
A-135 to A-149 (Town Houses & Duplexes)	1.03	1.02	.99	1.01	1.03	1.03
A-150 to A-162 (Urban Row Houses)	1.03	1.02	.99	1.01	1.03	1.02
A-163 to A-172 (Special Studies)	1.02	1.02	1.00	1.00	1.02	1.02
SECTION B						
B-1 to B-20 (Segregated Costs)	1.01	1.03	.99	1.02	1.00	1.01
SECTION C						
C-1 to C-12 (Yard Improvements)	1.01	1.02	1.00	1.00	1.02	1.02
C-13 to C-26 (Unit-in-Place)	1.01	1.02	1.00	1.00	1.02	1.02

LOCAL MULTIPLIERS

LOCAL MULTIPLIERS reflect local cost conditions and are designed to adjust the basic costs to each locality. They are based on weighted labor and material costs, including local sales taxes. In some cases, local building problems and practices must be considered. Refer to page F-9 for further discussion. They should always be combined with the Current Cost Multiplier to obtain a Cost Multiplier which will bring the costs to the present date and the locality of the estimate.

The data is received by us from sources we believe to be reliable, but no warranty, guaranty or representation is made by Marshall & Swift as to the correctness or sufficiency of any information, prices or representations contained in the RESIDENTIAL COST HANDBOOK, and Marshall & Swift assumes no responsibility or reliability in connection therewith.

EXAMPLE

After establishing a replacement cost from a preceding cost page, you should use both a Current Cost and a Local Multiplier. For this example, a Square Foot Method cost page for a wood frame, single family, detached residence has been used. The assumed Central District Current Cost Multiplier for "Frame" is 1.02. The Current Cost Multiplier will trend the costs on the Square Foot Method cost page to a current district average.

To adjust the cost to your location, a Local Multiplier should be used. For this example, the assumed location is Canton, Ohio. The Local Multiplier for "Frame" construction is assumed to be 1.05. If the cost from the Square Foot Method cost page is $50,000, the current cost for the residence in Canton, Ohio would be $53,550.

$50,000 × 1.02 × 1.05 = $53,550

DISTRICT MAP

WESTERN   CENTRAL   EASTERN

9/91
page F-1

Figure 5.4. Quarterly multipliers (Courtesy Marshall & Swift, Residential Cost Handbook, © 1991 Marshall & Swift).

A *site* is land which has been improved in some way. For example, trees may have been cleared, boulders removed, access roads constructed, or electric and water service provided. Generally, a site has greater value than a similar piece of raw land that has not yet been improved. A site may refer to only a portion of a parcel of land. When reviewing a property record card, one value for the site a home is built upon is often indicated, and a lower value, or values for other unimproved sections of the same parcel of land may be listed as well.

Some factors considered by appraisers when comparing a parcel of land with other parcels which have sold are:

LOCAL MULTIPLIERS

	FRAME	MASONRY		FRAME	MASONRY
CONNECTICUT	1.14	1.15	**IDAHO**	1.00	1.02
Bridgeport	1.23	1.23	Boise	1.05	1.06
Bristol	1.12	1.13	Caldwell	1.04	1.05
Danbury	1.24	1.22	Coeur d' Alene	1.01	1.05
Fairfield	1.22	1.22	Idaho Falls	.97	.96
Greenwich	1.37	1.35	Lewiston	.98	1.01
Hartford	1.18	1.19	Moscow	.99	1.01
Meriden	1.13	1.13	Pocatello	1.00	.99
Middletown	1.14	1.15	Twin Falls	1.04	1.04
Milford	1.14	1.14			
New Britain	1.14	1.15			
New Haven	1.14	1.16	**ILLINOIS**	1.07	1.06
New London	1.13	1.09	Alton	1.08	1.09
Norwich	1.12	1.09	Aurora	1.16	1.14
Stamford	1.37	1.35	Belleville	1.11	1.13
Waterbury	1.12	1.12	Bloomington	1.07	1.06
Windsor Locks	1.14	1.15	Carbondale	1.00	1.00
			Champaign	1.07	1.06
			Chicago	1.18	1.16
			Danville	1.07	1.06
DELAWARE	1.10	1.09	DeKalb	1.15	1.13
Dover	1.10	1.10	Decatur	1.06	1.05
Wilmington	1.11	1.10	East St. Louis	1.12	1.12
			Elgin	1.16	1.13
			Evanston	1.16	1.14
DIST. OF COLUMBIA	1.06	1.05	Galesburg	1.06	1.05
			Joliet	1.15	1.14
			Kankakee	1.18	1.14
			Marion	1.00	1.00
FLORIDA	.87	.87	Moline	1.07	1.05
Bradenton	.89	.87	Normal	1.07	1.06
Brevard Co.	.88	.87	Peoria	1.07	1.06
Broward Co.	.92	.92	Quincy	1.06	1.05
Dade Co.	.91	.91	Rock Island	1.07	1.05
Daytona Beach	.87	.87	Rockford	1.09	1.07
Fort Myers	.87	.87	Skokie	1.19	1.16
Fort Pierce	.87	.89	Springfield	1.08	1.07
Gainesville	.86	.86	Urbana	1.07	1.06
Jacksonville	.88	.87	Waukegan	1.15	1.14
Key West	1.04	1.06			
Lakeland	.90	.88			
Marathon	.98	.99	**INDIANA**	1.03	1.02
Miami	.91	.91	Anderson	1.07	1.05
Naples	.86	.84	Bloomington	1.04	1.04
Ocala	.86	.86	Columbus	1.05	1.05
Orlando	.91	.90	Elkhart	1.14	1.12
Palm Beach	.92	.92	Evansville	.96	.97
Panama City	.83	.84	Fort Wayne	1.04	1.04
Pensacola	.84	.85	Gary	1.15	1.13
Pinellas Co.	.89	.88	Hammond	1.15	1.13
Sarasota	.88	.85	Indianapolis	1.07	1.06
Tallahassee	.85	.85	Kokomo	1.06	1.03
Tampa	.88	.87	Lafayette	1.05	1.03
Vero Beach	.96	.87	Logansport	1.00	.99
			Marion	1.01	1.01
			Michigan City	1.14	1.12
GEORGIA	.87	.86	Muncie	1.04	1.04
Albany	.85	.84	Richmond	1.01	1.00
Athens	.88	.88	South Bend	1.13	1.11
Atlanta	.96	.94	Terre Haute	1.06	1.05
Augusta	.85	.84			
Columbus	.85	.85			
Macon	.88	.88	**IOWA**	.98	.98
Rome	.90	.90	Burlington	.98	.98
Savannah	.88	.87	Cedar Rapids	.96	.99
Valdosta	.85	.83	Council Bluffs	.94	.96
			Davenport	1.02	1.03
			Des Moines	.95	.96
			Dubuque	1.03	1.02
HAWAII	1.54	1.48	Fort Dodge	.96	.96
Hilo	1.55	1.49	Iowa City	.99	1.00
Kauai	1.56	1.49	Mason City	.96	.96
Maui	1.56	1.49	Sioux City	.97	.97
Oahu	1.54	1.48	Waterloo	.97	.98

Figure 5.5. Local multipliers (Courtesy Marshall & Swift, Residential Cost Handbook, © 1991 Marshall & Swift).

DEPRECIATION

TYPICAL BUILDING LIVES

Typical life expectancies of single and multi-family residences are based on case studies of both actual mortality and ages at which major reconstruction had taken place. The exceptions to the studies are the typical life expectancies for modular structures and manufactured housing (mobile homes). Typical life expectancies for modular structures assume conformity to site-built residences in both quality and design. Typical life expectancies for manufactured housing represent the projected mortality of structures produced after the enactment of more stringent local and national (U.S.) building codes. All cases of abnormal or excessive obsolescence due to external causes outside of and not inherent to the subject properties were excluded.

	SINGLE-FAMILY (Detached)			MULTI-FAMILY and SINGLE FAMILY (Attached)
	Site-built or modular:	Mfg. Housing: (mobile homes)		Site-built or modular:
QUALITY	Frame/Masonry	Single Wide	Multi Wide	Frame/Masonry
Low	40 / 45	20 / 25		....
Fair	45 / 50	20 / 25		40 / 45
Average	50 / 55	25 / 30		45 / 50
Good	50 / 55	30 / 35		45 / 50
Very Good	55 / 60	35 / 40		50 / 55
Excellent	55 / 60	40 / 45		....

USE OF THE TABLES

1. Determine the chronological age of the residence.
2. Compare the subject residence with like properties and study the affect of any modernization or major repair to determine Effective Age.
3. Determine Typical Life Expectancy from table above.
4. Enter the Depreciation Table in the column for the the appropriate life expectancy and at the Effective Age estimated in Step 2. The corresponding number is a normal percentage of depreciation.

CONDITION MODIFIER TABLE

The Depreciation Table is based on normal maintenance for structures of like type, age and occupancy. An adjustment may be necessary for above average or deferred maintenance if the appraiser chooses to treat condition separately. The Effective Age of a newer residence is usually the same as its chronological age and will not require a condition modification until those items subject to physical depreciation begin to show wear and are in need of repair.

EXCELLENT CONDITION - All items that can normally be repaired or refinished have recently been corrected, such as new roofing, new paint, furnace overhaul, etc. .... X .80

VERY GOOD CONDITION - All items well maintained, many having been overhauled and repaired as they showed signs of wear .... X .85

GOOD CONDITION - No obvious maintenance required but neither is everything new. .... X .90

AVERAGE CONDITION - Some evidence of deferred maintenance in that a few minor repairs and refinishing are needed. .... X 1.00

BADLY WORN - Much repair needed. Many items need refinishing or overhauling. .... X 1.10

WORN OUT - Repair and overhaul needed on painted surfaces, roofing, plumbing, heating, etc. (Found only in extraordinary circumstances.) .... X 1.15

EXAMPLE

The subject residence is a Good Quality, wood frame, single-family, detached residence. From inspection of the residence and through comparison to other similar residences, the appraiser has determined that the Effective Age and the chronological age for the subject and the neighborhood are equal and is 20 years.

The Typical Life Expectancy from the above table is 50 years. From the Depreciation Table, the percentage of depreciation is 22%. Since the subject residence was in some what better condition than average for the area, a condition modifier for Good Condition at .90 is used in place of lowering the overall effective age. This modifier is multiplied by the percentage of depreciation to estimate a net depreciation of 19.8% (.90 x 22% = 19.8%). Rounded, this represents a 20% depreciation at a 50 year life.

Referring again to the Depreciation Table to compare the modified effective age after applying a condition modifier, the net depreciation of 20% is that of a residence having an effective age of 19 years instead of a 20 year effective age which was found to be typical of the neighborhood.

Figure 5.6. Depreciation schedules (Courtesy Marshall & Swift, Residential Cost Handbook, © 1991 Marshall & Swift).

1. *Size:* Is the parcel fairly similar in size to the comparable parcels? If the comparable parcels are too large or too small they probably don't relate well to the value of the subject parcel.

2. *Site vs raw land:* Is the subject parcel an improved site, or raw land? If it is a site, it should be compared with other improved sites, or else some adjustments to the sales prices of the comparable parcels must be made.

3. *Zoning:* Are the comparable parcels zoned the same as the subject parcel? If not, their uses may be limited, affecting their value as comparable parcels.

DEPRECIATION

TYPICAL LIFE EXPECTANCY IN YEARS

Effective Age In Years	15	20	25	30	35	40	45	50	55	60	Effective Age In Years
					DEPRECIATION - PERCENTAGE						
1	5%	4%	3%	3%	3%	2%	1%	1%	0%	0%	1
2	9	7	6	6	5	4	2	1	1	1	2
3	14	11	8	8	8	6	3	2	2	2	3
4	18	14	11	10	10	7	4	3	2	2	4
5	22	17	13	12	12	8	5	4	3	3	5
6	26	20	16	14	14	10	6	5	4	4	6
7	30	23	18	16	15	12	7	6	5	5	7
8	33	26	21	19	17	13	8	7	6	6	8
9	37	29	23	21	19	15	9	8	7	6	9
10	41	32	25	23	21	16	11	9	8	7	10
11	45	35	27	25	23	18	12	10	9	8	11
12	48	37	29	26	24	19	13	11	10	9	12
13	52	40	32	28	26	21	14	12	11	10	13
14	55	43	34	30	28	23	16	13	12	11	14
15	59	46	37	32	30	24	17	15	13	12	15
16	63	48	39	34	31	26	19	16	14	13	16
17	66	51	41	36	33	28	20	17	16	14	17
18		54	44	38	34	29	22	19	17	16	18
19		57	46	40	35	30	24	20	18	17	19
20		60	48	41	37	31	25	22	20	18	20
21		63	50	43	39	33	26	24	21	19	21
22		66	52	45	41	35	28	25	22	20	22
23			55	47	42	36	30	26	24	21	23
24			57	49	44	37	32	28	25	23	24
25			61	51	46	39	33	30	27	24	25
26			63	52	47	40	35	32	28	25	26
27			65	54	49	42	36	33	29	27	27
28				56	50	43	38	35	31	28	28
29				58	52	45	40	36	33	29	29
30				60	54	46	41	38	34	31	30
31				62	55	48	42	40	36	32	31
32				63	56	49	44	42	38	33	32
33				65	58	51	46	44	39	35	33
34					59	52	48	45	41	36	34
35					61	53	49	46	42	37	35
36					62	54	51	48	43	39	36
37					64	56	53	49	45	40	37
38					66	57	54	51	46	41	38
39						59	55	52	47	41	39
40						60	56	53	49	43	40
41						62	57	54	50	45	41
42						63	58	56	51	46	42
43						63	59		52	47	43
44						64	60	58	54	48	44
45						65	61	58	55	49	45
46							61	59	56	50	46
47							62	60	57	51	47
48							63	61	58	52	48
49							64	61	58	53	49
50							65	62	59	54	50
51								62	60	55	51
52								63	61	56	52
53								64	61	57	53
54								64	62	58	54
55									62	59	55
56									62	59	56
57									63	60	57
58									63	61	58
59									64	62	59
60									64	62	60
61									65	63	61
62										63	62
63										64	63
64										64	64
65										64	65

Figure 5.7. Building life expectancy table (Courtesy Marshall & Swift, Residential Cost Handbook, © 1991 Marshall & Swift).

4. *Time:* How long ago did the sales of the comparable parcels take place? If they sold several years ago the sales prices may no longer reflect their current value.

5. *Topography and other physical characteristics:* Is the subject parcel similar in character to the comparable parcels? For example, a very steeply graded, heavily wooded lot may differ greatly in value from a level, grassy lot, and would not be a good comparable.

6. *Location:* Are the locations of the comparable parcels similar, better, or worse than the subject property? Waterfront or other prime location property is worth more than property in a less desireable location.

Various sources of land sales information can be used to verify the accuracy of the tax assessor's computation of value for a parcel of land. The first place to look is in the assessor's office itself. Many assessing offices maintain updated lists of all property sales which have occurred within their jurisdiction. These lists will sometimes supply all the comparable sales information needed. If such a list is not available, ask the assessor which specific sales were used for comparison purposes, so that the sales data may be verified.

Other sources of sales information include:

1. County records of deeds (often located at county courthouse).
2. Real estate brokers and agents (Multiple Listing Service).
3. Commercial sales reporting services.
4. Appraisers.
5. Lawyers.
6. Banks.
7. Newspaper advertisements.
8. Title reporting companies.
9. Federal Housing Administration (FHA) office.
10. Mortgage companies.
11. Personal knowledge of sales from neighbors or friends.
12. Municipal planning or engineering commissions.

Valuing land based on sales prices of other parcels

Let's now consider how land is valued when using the cost approach. In particular, we will look at how a tax assessor might adjust comparable land-sale values that, for one reason or another, are not perfectly suited for comparison with the subject property. Remember that various factors such as topography, location, time at which sale occurred, and zoning (among others) can all affect the value relationship that a comparable land sale has to a subject property. If there are significant differences between the subject site and a comparable site, adjustments to the sales price of the comparable site must be made. If not, the sales price of the comparable site will not truly reflect the value of the subject site.

When an adjustment to value is made, it is always made to the comparable site and never to the subject. Remember that the objective is to determine a value for the subject site. If the comparable site has a deficiency of some kind, the sales price is adjusted upward to reflect what it would have sold for if the deficiency did not exist. If the comparable site is better than the subject in some way, the sales price is adjusted downward to reflect what the sales price would have been if the site was not better than the subject.

Example of how adjustments to land value are made.   A simplified example will clarify this. To determine the value of an acre of land (the "subject"), sales of three different comparable acres that occurred in the recent past are examined. The properties are described as follows:

The subject acre is square shaped, hilly, and covered with grass and widely scattered trees.

Acre A is irregular in shape, hilly, and covered with grass and widely scattered trees. It sold for $15,000.

Acre B is square shaped, hilly, and covered with grass and widely scattered trees. It sold for $18,000.

Acre C is square shaped, flat, and covered with grass and widely scattered trees. It sold for $21,000.

The adjustments to value of the comparable sales, as illustrated in Table 5.1 are now described.

Acre A is similar to the subject acre, except that it is irregular in shape. If it was square (like the subject), it would be worth more. We will adjust its value upwards by $3,000, pretending, in effect, that it is more like the subject acre. Its adjusted sales price is $18,000.

Acre B seems to match the subject acre very closely and is a good comparable. No adjustment is needed to its $18,000 sales price.

Acre C is better than the subject acre because it is flat and requires no grading. It's sales price is lowered by $3,000 to reflect what it would have sold for if it was hilly, like the subject acre. Its' adjusted sales price would be $18,000.

The concluded adjusted price of $18,000 for the comparable acres reflects the probable price of the subject acre. By adjusting for the differences between the subject acre and acres A and C, making them, in effect, more like the subject, a better value relationship is established.

The same process used for adjusting sales prices of comparable land sales is used for adjusting comparable building sales as well. In Chap. 6, "The Market Data Approach," we will see how adjustments are made to home sales prices when appraisers use the market data approach to property valuation.

Finding Errors in a Tax Assessor's Cost Valuation

We have said that there are pitfalls awaiting anyone who trusts blindly in the cost approach. There are a number of ways in which inaccurate property values may result with incorrect usage of this method. The types of mass appraisals that are practiced in many towns and cities, in this country particularly, lend themselves

Table 5.1. Adjustments to Value of Comparable Sales

	Shape	Topography	Vegetation	Sale Price	Adjustment	Adjusted Price
Acre A	Irregular	Hilly	Grass/trees	$15,000	+ $3,000	$18,000
Acre B	Square	Hilly	Grass/trees	$18,000	—	$18,000
Acre C	Square	Flat	Grass/trees	$21,000	− $3,000	$18,000
Subject	Square	Hilly	Grass/trees	—	—	—

to these inaccuracies. With a basic understanding of how a cost-approach property valuation is done, it is possible to spot and correct valuation errors before they are reflected in an unnecessarily high tax bill. The most typical kinds of errors assessors make when using the cost approach fall into the following groups:

- *Mathematical errors:* The computations of value, using base square-foot costs and any adjustment multipliers contained on the property record card, should be checked for accuracy. Decimal points get shifted, figures get transposed, and simple addition and subtraction is done improperly. The math used on property record cards is usually fairly straightforward and can be checked quickly with a calculator.

- *Mechanical errors:* These are errors in measurement of various types, or simple typos or copying errors in the assessor's records. A clerk may omit or incorrectly record property data. The total land area or the area of the house itself may be incorrect. Often a sketch of the home on the property record card will include the assessor's measurements of the home. These figures should be checked for accuracy by actually measuring the home.

- *Gross description errors:* At times, descriptions of features of a home are in error. Such things as the style and condition of a home, the number of stories, the number of rooms, or the addition of special features such as decks and pools are described incorrectly. All of these types of errors can result in incorrect value assessments by the tax assessor.

- *Land valuation errors:* These are incorrect conclusions of land value, usually listed on a property record card in two ways: as a value per square foot or per acre, and as a total dollar value for the complete parcel. Incorrect land values can result when the assessor compares the value of your land with inappropriate comparable land sales. Did he or she use comparable sales from too long ago? Are the comparable parcels much too large or too small in comparison with yours? Do other factors make the comparable land sales poor choices to compare with your land?

In our final example, we will illustrate how a cost-approach valuation might appear in an assessor's records. Pretend it is your property assessment that you are reviewing. Remember, like all methods of valuing property, the cost approach results in an opinion of value. Based on what you know about the cost approach so far, try to consider some of the ways in which you might disagree with the assessor's opinion of value in the following example. In particular, look at each item on the property record card with an eye towards how you could verify its accuracy.

Description of property

The subject home is a 30-year-old ranch. It has three bedrooms, a den, living room, kitchen, and 1½ bathrooms located in the main rectangular section of the house. A family room addition measuring 14 × 10 ft was added several years ago to the back of the house, leading to a screened-in, unheated porch area measuring 14 × 20 ft. A two-car attached garage is located at one end of the house, measuring 29 × 18 ft.

The home is in generally good repair, reflecting its age, however, in a number of areas. The asphalt shingle roof, replaced 10 years earlier, will need to be replaced again soon. The painted wood shingles on the home's exterior are in need of repainting, and a number of them are cracked and should be replaced. All of the windows date to the original construction of the home. Although they have been caulked and painted regularly, they are not as efficient as more modern designs, and will likely need replacement in coming years.

In general, the floor plan of the home is good, without any undesirable design flaws. The rooms are large sized, and the interior finish is mostly of good quality. Most rooms contain wall-to-wall carpeting in good condition, expected to last another 3 to 5 years before needing replacement. The full basement has not been finished, although about a quarter of it has been turned into a partially finished work area.

The heating system has recently been upgraded from an oil to a gas burning design. Individual room air conditioners are located in all three bedrooms and the living room. The energy efficiency of the home is average for its age and style, which is to say, it is not as good as more modern homes incorporating the latest in energy-efficient designs.

According to the property deed, the lot is square shaped, extending for 250 ft on each side. Its size is fairly typical of other lots in the neighborhood. It is located near the beginning of a street that, in the past two years, has been extended to accommodate a new housing development. The neighborhood is in good condition and has been improving, most noticeably with the addition of the latest section of new homes.

With this general picture of the property in mind, let's look at how the local property tax records describe the home. The property record card, shown in Figs. 5.8 and 5.9, was recently completed following a revaluation of all properties in the tax district. Like most property record cards, this one requires you to look carefully to find the information you will want to check. Property record cards tend to pack a lot of information into a small area. A calculator will be useful in checking the figures.

Let's examine the property record card example with an eye towards finding the four main types of errors most likely to occur when an assessor uses the cost approach: *mathematical errors, mechanical errors, gross description errors,* and land valuation errors.

Step 1: Check for mathematical errors. Although there is no particular order in which to examine a property record card, let's start with a check of the square-foot area computations performed by the assessor, as shown on the sketch of the home. The square-foot area of each main portion of the house is computed separately and circled. The figure "1950," circled in the middle of the sketch, is arrived at by multiplying the length of the main living section (65 ft) by its width

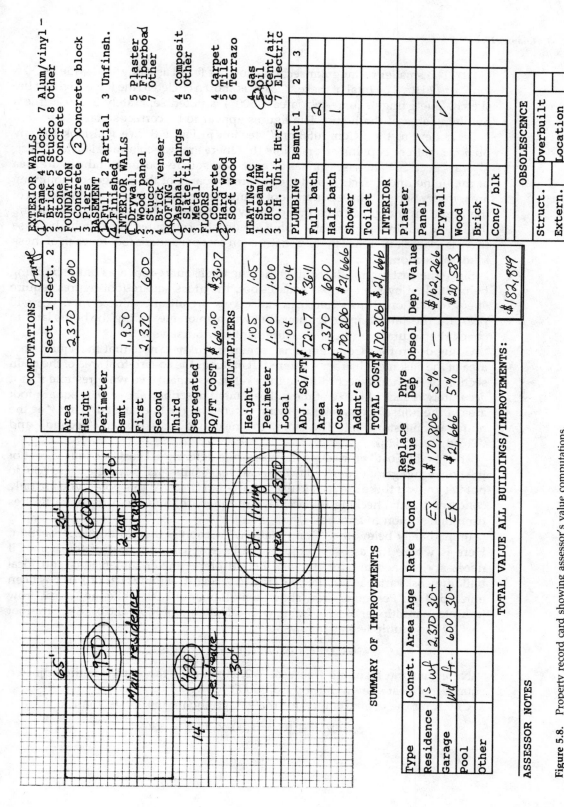

Figure 5.8. Property record card showing assessor's value computations.

(30 ft). The smaller rectangular section shown is listed as being 14 ft wide by 30 ft long, or 420 ft². The total of these, "2370" is shown circled to the lower right of the sketch. The garage square-foot area ("600") is noted separately because it is a nonliving area of the home. The figures appear to be correct so far.

Refer next to the "Computations" section in Fig. 5.8. We will look for any obvious math or copying errors. Note that there are two columns, labeled "Sect. 1" and "Sect. 2." The assessor has recorded the square-foot area of the living area of the home under Sect. 1, and the square-foot area of the garage, or nonliving area, under Sect. 2. These square-foot figures were transferred from the sketch of the home on the graph area immediately to the left. The costs of constructing living and nonliving areas of a home are usually computed separately, because there is a large difference in the construction cost per square-foot for each of these kinds of sections.

Since the cost approach requires that the total square-foot area of the building be multiplied by the cost per square-foot, the gross square-foot figures require special attention. Errors here can cause very significant value errors. We will presume they are accurate for now, but will plan on measuring the home later to check the accuracy of these measurements for ourselves.

Going down the "Computations" columns, we next note that the square-foot area of the basement has been entered. It matches the square-foot area of the main section of the house according to the sketch, so, again, we will presume that it accurately reflects the size of the full basement described above. The square-foot area of the house and garage are again entered on the line labeled "First," as the house is one story tall. Therefore, the next two lines labeled "Second" and "Third," are blank.

The "Sq/Ft Cost" entries are the assessor's determined cost per square-foot of the house and garage, derived from whatever cost manual he or she uses. You do not yet know if these are reasonable square-foot costs. At this point, you are only concerned with checking the accuracy of the math, and the carrying of figures from one section to another.

Immediately below the "Computations" section is the "Multipliers" section. Here is where the assessor adjusts the base square-foot cost of the home, if necessary, to account for unusual height or perimeter dimensions and local building-cost variables. In the row labeled "Height" a multiplier of 1.05 has been entered. The "Perimeter" row shows a multiplier of 1.00, while the "Local" row indicates a multiplier of 1.04. Using your calculator, multiply the base square-foot cost by the multipliers as follows:

$$\$66.00 \times 1.05 \times 1.00 \times 1.04 = \$72.07$$

Note that the resulting figure of $72.07 matches the entry for the adjusted square-foot cost shown in the "Adj. Sq/Ft" row.

Checking the computations for the garage square-foot costs you find:

$$\$33.07 \times 1.05 \times 1.00 \times 1.04 = \$36.11$$

Continuing to work down the "Multipliers" section, the next calculations to check are those recorded in the "Cost" row. Multiply the "Adj. Sq/Ft" entry by the "Area" as shown:

$$2370 \text{ ft}^2 \times \$72.07 = \$170,806 \qquad \text{(house)}$$

$$600 \text{ ft}^2 \times \$36.11 = \$21,666 \qquad \text{(garage)}$$

So far, it appears that the property record card figures are accurate. Note that you haven't yet verified the validity of the square-foot costs or of the multipliers, any of which could be inappropriate for this property. You have only checked the simple math.

Continuing down the property record card, you come to a section titled "Summary of Improvements." Under the column entitled "Replace Value," the figures representing the replacement cost new for the house and garage are carried over from the "Multipliers" section. They match, so no copying error has occurred. The assessor has listed a depreciation of 5 percent for both the house and garage, shown in the "Phys Dep" column. Multiplying the replacement value by the reciprocal of the depreciation amount will result in the depreciated value of the property, shown in the "Dep. Value" column. Check these figures on your calculator as shown:

$$\$170,806 \times 0.95 = \$162,266 \qquad \text{(house)}$$

$$\$21,666 \times 0.95 = \$20,583 \qquad \text{(garage)}$$

The sum of the depreciated value of the house and garage should match the figure recorded in the field labeled "Total Value All Buildings/Improvements," and in fact it does:

$$\$162,266 + \$20,583 = \$182,849$$

The last figures to check are found in Fig. 5.9. In the section entitled "Assessment Record," recheck the "Total Land & Building" sum by adding the land and building values together. The "Total Value Building" figure should match the total "Dep. Value" amount computed in Fig. 5.9. The "Total Value Land" amount (Fig. 5.9) should match the "Totals" figure, found in the "Land Value Computations and Summary" section immediately below it.

Notice, in the "Land Value Computations and Summary" section (Fig. 5.9), that the assessor has recorded the land size as ".69 ac" for the primary site, and "1.04 ac" for the secondary site. Assessors normally record either the total square-foot area of each portion of a parcel of land *or* the total acreage, as in this case. To check the assessor's computations of land value, multiply the acreage of the primary site by the rate (per acre) as shown:

$$0.69 \text{ acre} \times \$40,000 = \$27,600$$

Parcel #: 032-232-000

56 Henning Drive

OWNER: Ronald & Elisa Smith
56 Henning Drive
Anywhere, NH 00232

RECORD OF OWNERSHIP	DATE	BOOK	PAGE	PRICE	Class	RES
Ricci, Salvatore	04-18-79	11231	317	$149,500	Zoning	R1
Aaron, James + René	11-07-84	19120	191	$174,000	Use	SFR
Smith, Ronald + Elisa	06-15-89	22071	214	$202,500	NH Code	RES

ASSESSMENT RECORD

INSPECTION WITNESSED BY:

	19 81	19 86	19 91	19	Visit History
Building	105,000	124,480	162,269		Jensen, P. 9-15-81
Garage/Non-living	10,000	15,580	20,586		Harvey, J. 9-1-86
Other	-	-	-		Harvey, J. 9-25-91
TOTAL VALUE BUILDING	115,000	140,000	182,855		
TOTAL VALUE LAND	40,000	55,000	68,480		
TOTAL LAND & BUILDING	156,000	195,000	251,335		

LAND VALUE COMPUTATIONS AND SUMMARY

Description	Code	Size	Rate	Influence Factor	Land Value
Primary site	R1	.69 ac	$40,000	+20%	$33,120
Secondary site	RU1	1.04 ac	$34,000		$35,360
Undeveloped					
Marshland					
Waterfront					
TOTALS					$68,480

NOTES:

Property Factors

TOPOGRAPHY		STREET	
Level	✓	Paved	✓
Hilly		Sidewalk	
Swampy		Unpaved	
NEIGHBORHOOD		**IMPROVEMENTS**	
Improving	✓	Water	✓
Static		Electric	✓
Declining		Sewer	✓

Figure 5.9a.   Property record card (front).

Increase the resulting figure by the amount of the influence factor shown for the primary site, to arrive at the figure shown in the "Land Value" column:

$$\$27,600 \times 1.2 = \$33,120 \text{ (primary site)}$$

Doing the same for the secondary site we get:

$$1.04 \text{ acre} \times \$34,000 = \$35,360 \text{ (secondary site)}$$

The total value of the primary and secondary sites is $68,480, and this amount is entered correctly in both the "Assessment Record" section and the "Land Value Computations and Summary" section. All figures appear accurate so far, and no obvious math or copying errors have been detected.

Step 2: Check for mechanical errors. When looking for so-called mechanical, or measurement errors, start with the assessor's sketch of the house. You will need to perform your own exterior measurement of your home. In our example, we will assume that you do so, and that your measurements point out some errors.

Refer to Fig. 5.10, which represents your actual measurements of the house. Compare it with the assessor's measurements, as shown in Fig. 5.8. The first error noted is in the size of the garage. It actually measures 29' × 18 ft, for a total of 522 ft^2. Secondly, your measurement of the main portion of the house shows it is 29 × 63 ft, for a total of 1827 ft^2. The family room located in the smaller back section of the home is 14 × 10 ft, or 140 ft^2. Attached to the family room is a 14 × 20 ft screened-in porch that should have been listed on the property record card as a nonliving area. Instead, the property record card incorrectly depicts the family

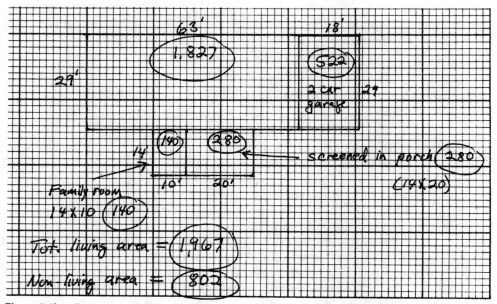

Figure 5.9b. Property record card (back).

room and screened-in porch as one large 14 × 30 ft section of living area. Properly separated, the corrected total square-foot area of both living and nonliving areas should be:

Living area

Main House   *Family Room*

(63 × 29 ft) + (14 × 10 ft) =
1827 ft^2 + 140 ft^2 = 1967 ft^2

Nonliving area

Garage   Screened-in Porch

(29 × 18 ft) + (14 × 20 ft) =
522 ft^2 + 280 ft^2 = 802 ft^2

Using the corrected total area figures, and the assessor's square-foot costs of $72.07 and $36.11 for living and nonliving areas, respectively, the measurement errors, by themselves, translate into an assessing error of $20,663 as shown:

Living area

		Corrected Value	*Assessor's Value*
1967 ft^2 × $72.07	=	$141,762	
(Depreciated 5%)	=	$134,674	$162,266

Nonliving area

802 ft^2 × $36.11	=	$ 28,960	
(Depreciated 5%)	=	$27,512	$ 20,583
Totals		$162,186	$182,849

$182,849 − $162,186 = $20,663 assessing error

The next measurement to check is the size of the land, as shown on the property record card. While it may not always be practical to physically measure a large parcel, you should at least review the description of your land as it appears on your property deed. If you cannot locate a copy of this document at home, you should be able to get a replacement wherever property deeds are recorded (often a county courthouse) in your area.

Recall in the description of this property that the deed indicates a square-shaped lot extending for 250 ft on each side, for a total of 62,500 ft^2. The assessor has recorded a primary site size of 0.69 acre, and a secondary site size of 1.04 acres (Fig. 5.9). The total parcel is, therefore, listed as 1.73 acres. To translate this figure into square feet, multiply by 43,560 ft^2 (one acre):

$$1.73 \times 43,560 = 75,359 \text{ ft}^2$$

The assessor, therefore, has listed the parcel as being 12,859 ft^2, or 0.295 acres larger than the property deed shows. If the deed is correct (and it's worth measuring the parcel now to find out), this represents an assessing error of about $10,000, based on the secondary site land value of $34,000 an acre.

$$0.295 \times \$34,000 = \$10,030$$

Combined with the house measurement errors, a total valuation error of $30,693 has been found so far.

Step 3: Check for gross description errors. After checking for math and measurement errors, examine every entry on the property record card looking for errors in the description of the property. Property record cards vary greatly in design, and assessors vary greatly in how they complete the cards. It isn't uncommon to find cards with many data fields left blank, or with cryptic notes scribbled in the margins that, at first glance, appear indecipherable. When studying your own property record card, make notes of items which aren't clear to you, for later discussion with the assessor.

Looking at Fig. 5.8, we note that the assessor has described the basement as full, which is correct, but has also indicated it is a finished basement, which is not true, based on our property description. In the "Plumbing" section, the assessor indicates the house has two full baths and one half bath, compared with the actual number of one full bath and one half bath. There is no way to tell, from the card, how these items have affected the final value determination, but they should be noted for future discussion with the assessor.

The condition of the residence and garage in the "Summary of Improvements" section are described as "EX," or excellent. However, from the property description, we know that there are a number of major items, such as the roof and exterior walls, that are showing some wear. This home is more likely in good, or average condition for its age. Again, make a note of this item for discussion with the assessor, since it will affect his or her overall opinion of value.

One of the more glaring descriptive errors in Fig. 5.8 is the amount of depreciation listed for the house and garage. A 30-year-old home in good condition would be expected to depreciate more than 5 percent, especially with the kind of wear and tear noted in the property description. A good case could be made for increasing the depreciation amount in a meeting with the assessor. Depreciation tables contained in cost manuals describe "average" depreciation amounts for typical properties. If your property has more deficiencies than average, you may be able to make a case for increasing the amount of depreciation shown for the property, lowering its assessed value.

There are several other descriptive errors listed on the property record in our example. We will leave it to you to find them. When you review your own property record card, your knowledge of your home will make the process of spotting descriptive errors that much easier.

Step 4: Check for land valuation errors. For this step, you will need to have a reasonably good idea of what land is selling for in your neighborhood. If you disagree with the assessor's value for your land, you will have to produce some evidence of why his or her figures are wrong. In our example, the assessor values the primary site at $40,000 an acre, and the secondary site at $34,000 an acre.

How could you research these values? You could ask the assessor how the figures where arrived at, and would probably be given a list of several relevant property sales. Call local real estate agents or appraisers, or look in the real estate section of the newspaper for sales prices. Look, also, at some property record cards for neighboring properties to see if the rates shown on your property record card are similar to theirs. Remember that factors such as location, size, and quality of the land may affect its value, so expect some variations among the value of your neighbors' land as reflected on their property record cards.

Step 5: Prepare list of miscellaneous questions for assessor. Prepare a list of questions for the assessor for all items on the property record card which are unclear. Ask how the specific base square-foot costs and multipliers were determined for your property. If they appear much different from those used for neighbors' homes of similar size, construction, and age, ask why. Ask if all known deficiencies in your home were accounted for in the assessor's opinion of value, in particular if you feel the number and type of deficiencies are greater than is typical of similar homes. Can a larger depreciation percentage be applied to your property because of excess wear and tear? In general, this is your opportunity to clarify all miscellaneous grey areas concerning your property assessment.

Summary

This chapter has described the cost approach to valuing real property. The cost approach determines the cost of replacing or reproducing a structure on land of similar value to the subject property, accounting for depreciation of the existing structure.

Buildings lose value over time due to depreciation, which may be caused by wear and tear or obsolescence. Obsolescence may be functional or external, and may be curable or incurable depending upon its cause.

The cost approach may utilize different methods of estimating cost. The comparative unit method is the most common method used by tax assessors when valuing residential properties. Cost manuals are available which organize cost data for use with the comparative unit method. Other cost estimation methods include the segregated cost and quantity survey methods.

Land is valued separately from buildings when using the cost approach. Land is never depreciated. A site is land which has been improved in some way. Various factors may affect the value of a parcel of land, including location, size, zoning, and topography. Tax assessors usually value land by analyzing sales prices of comparable parcels of land.

The most common errors made by tax assessors using the cost approach to value residential properties are mathematical errors, mechanical errors, gross description errors, and land valuation errors.

6

The Market-Data Approach

Grace is given of God, but knowledge is bought in the market.
ARTHUR HUGH CLOUGH (1819–1861)

The market-data approach is the most commonly used method for appraising residential properties. The market-data approach is based on the economic principle of substitution. This principle asserts that the market value of a product or service tends to be set by the cost of obtaining a similar product or service, assuming that substitute is available in the marketplace.

With residential properties, this means that the value of a property tends to be set by the prices paid for similar properties.

The market-data approach measures the actions of buyers and sellers in the marketplace. It makes a direct comparison between a subject property and similar properties that have recently sold in the marketplace. It makes use of the concept of market value.

When you use the market-data approach, you will select homes that are similar to your own home. In the rest of this chapter, we will refer to these homes that you select as comparable sales, comparable homes, or comparable properties.

Market Value

As mentioned earlier, ""Market value is an estimate of the price that a property would likely bring if offered for sale on the open market by a knowledgeable, willing seller to a knowledgeable, willing buyer." You must know what the market value of your home is before you can show that your tax assessment is unequal or excessive.

In considering market value, the following elements always affect the value of a home:

1. *Property rights conveyed:* Recall from Chap. 2 that ownership of property confers certain rights, such as the rights to enter and use the property, sell it, lease it, or not use it at all. In real-property discussions, these and other rights are referred to as the "bundle of rights." Ownership may include all or only a portion of the total number of rights.

The property rights conveyed with most single family residences are "fee-simple" rights. When you choose comparable sales, make sure that the ownership rights transferred in the sale are comparable to the ownership rights you possess in your property. If they aren't, locate another comparable sale to use.

2. *Financing terms:* Most sales of private homes involve the buyer placing some money down and financing the rest with some type of mortgage. If the comparable sales you choose involve normal financing arrangements, the effects of the financing on the property value will be typical of the market. However, if unusual financing terms are involved, they can distort the value relationship that you are trying to demonstrate with your home.

An anxious owner, financing the entire selling price without any down payment, is an example of unusual financing. An adjustment would be necessary to compensate for the effects of this financing.

Such adjustments are not easily made and are outside of the scope of this book. When you choose comparable sales, make sure that the financing terms are typical of sales in your area. If they aren't, locate another comparable sale to use.

3. *Conditions of the sale:* A comparable sale should be "at arm's length." This means that the buyer and the seller were knowledgeable about the market value of the sale and were under no compulsion to buy or sell at other than market value.

An owner in need of emergency cash who is willing to sell below market value, or an intrafamily sale where a parent is selling to a child below market value would not be considered "arm's length" sales. When you choose comparable sales, determine if the sale was at "arm's length." If it wasn't, locate another comparable sale to use.

To simplify the process, select comparable sales that involve fee-simple title, that have typical financing terms, and that are at "arm's length." If you do so, you will not need to make adjustments for these elements.

Comparable sales will almost always need adjustments for the next three elements.

4. *Location:* How often have you heard it said that the three most important factors to consider when buying real estate are location, location, and location? While the phrase may be overused, it is emphatically true. It indicates the important role that location plays in the value of any property.

The comparable sales you choose should have locations similar to your property.

Your task is to find comparable properties located in an area like your neighborhood. Closeness is not enough. For example, a home two blocks from yours is close. But if it's on a busy road and your home is on a quiet dead-end street, its location will affect its value compared with your property. And another property two blocks away may be positively affected if it happens to be waterfront real estate.

Other location characteristics can affect the value of seemingly similar properties. These include zoning differences, the availability of public utilities, public services, or schools.

So it's possible that the homes most similar to your own, in terms of location, may be in an area some distance away. Usually, however, you should be able to find good comparable properties close to home.

5. *Date of sale:* In selecting comparable properties, the more recent the sale, the better it will support your case. A house sold five years ago was sold under a very different set of economic conditions than exist today. At that time, mortgage rates, inflation, availability of homes, local and global economic factors, tax law changes, and other factors may have produced a considerably different market.

The closer a sale is to the present, the more it relates to current market values. Of course events such as a stock market crash could affect home values immediately. However, such events are not typical of the more gradual trends that drive the marketplace over time.

In a good market, with sales occurring frequently and prices going up quickly, look for comparable sales that occurred in the past six months or less.

In a slower market, you can use comparable properties that sold further back. A two-year-old sale might be acceptable to an assessor reviewing your comparable sales approach.

6. *Physical features:* This is probably the area in which you'll do the most adjusting to the values of comparable sales. It includes any physical aspect of the property which contributes to value. Physical features include square-foot area, number of rooms, style of construction, and level of craftsmanship. It also includes special features like pools, decks, patios, custom landscaping, and finished basements.

There can be a great number of differences between your property and the comparable properties that you select. Try to select comparable properties as similar to your own home as possible.

For example, if your home is a ranch, try to find ranch style comparable properties with features similar to your own home. If your home doesn't have a swimming pool and a deck, make an effort to find ranches without a pool and a deck.

Basic Steps in the Market-Data Approach

There are three basic steps in the market-data approach. They are:

1. Locate recently sold comparable properties.
2. Contrast the comparable homes to the subject property and make adjustments to the sales price of the comparable homes to compensate for any important differences between the subject and the comparable homes.
3. Reconcile the differences and determine the value of the subject, based on the adjusted sales prices of the comparable properties.

Step 1: Locating recently sold comparable properties. Your success with this method depends on the comparable homes that you select. The best comparable properties to choose are those that are very similar to your home. They should be close in age, design, square-foot area, type of neighborhood, location, and special features. It won't do you any good to compare your 1500 ft^2, cape-style home to a 3500 ft^2 tudor with three more bedrooms, located in a better neighborhood.

The sales you select should also be zoned similarly to yours. Normally, homes are zoned for residential use, but some are zoned for limited commercial use as well. For instance, a professional might have a practice in his or her home that has been specially zoned for such use. The home's value will be affected by the difference in zoning.

Remember, your task is to select properties as similar to your own as possible and then to account for all the important differences through adjustments.

You need to locate a minimum of five homes, similar to yours, that have sold within the past year, preferably, within the last six months. The more recent the sale is, the better it indicates current market value.

The homes that you select as comparable sales should be reasonably similar to your home in size, design, type of construction, physical condition, and location. If your home is a colonial, compare it with other colonials. If your home is a ranch, compare it with other ranches.

Be sure to get front-view photographs of the comparable sales.

Get the date of sale, the actual sale price, and the name of the legal owner for each of the comparable homes you select. It's important that you verify as much of the information as possible. Determine, if you can, what property rights were conveyed, what the financing terms were, and if the sale was at "arm's length." Property record cards sometimes contain this type of information. You might even be able to contact the buyers and sellers or the real estate agent involved in the sale to check this data.

If you don't know of any recent sales, some sources for this information are:

- *Local real estate agent:* Find an agent who belongs to a multiple listing service. A multiple listing service provides, among other things, computerized listings of houses that have sold, or have been offered for sale, within the past six months or year. These listings are by neighborhood or development, and provide detailed physical description, sales, and mortgage information. Real estate agents will often give you the comparable information you need in the expectation that when you decide to sell your home and buy another, you'll do business with them.

- *The tax assessor's office:* Your tax assessor will generally use the market-data approach in determining the assessed value of your home. Ask for the comparable sales used by the assessor. He or she will provide you with this public information to prove to you that the assessment is fair. Ask for information on other homes that you think are better comparable properties if you are aware of some.

- *The county record office or registry of deeds:* They contain specific sales information. Be prepared to sort through many different types of records to find what you need. The transfer-tax stamps on deeds may provide sales price information;

however, this may not be accurate. Check to see if the amount indicated on the tax stamp is the total price to purchase the house and not, for example, only the amount of cash paid at the closing.

Other sources of information are:

- Federal Housing Administration (FHA) or Veterans Administration (VA) offices
- Title insurance offices
- Local banks
- Local newspapers
- Real estate appraisers may also have the information you need, but may charge for it. (After all, it is their business.)

Step 2: Adjusting the sale prices of the comparable properties. An adjustment is a technique to compensate for the differences between your home (the subject home) and the comparable homes you select. As you adjust the known market values of the comparable homes to your own home, their adjusted values help indicate the value of your home.

Your home is the basis for any adjustment. Adjustments are never made to your home. Adjustments are always made to the comparable sales to make them more like your home.

If your home is better than a comparable home with respect to an item, adjust the sale price of the comparable home upward to make it more like your home.

If your home is inferior to a comparable home with respect to an item, adjust the sale price of the comparable home downward to make it more like your home.

For example, suppose your home has a fireplace and a comparable home doesn't. Adjust the comparable home's sales price upwards by the amount of value you believe a fireplace would add. By doing this, you are making the comparable home more like your home.

Remember, never adjust the value of your home (the subject). Instead, adjust the value of the comparable you're using. How to do this will become clear to you in the following examples, based on the information below. The examples are summarized in Table 6.1.

How to adjust for value. You live on Elm Street and you want to determine the value of your home for an appeal of your assessment. You have found four homes similar to your own that you plan to use in an appeal. House A, on Elm Street, is

Table 6.1. Example: Making Adjustments to Sales Prices

House	Street	Time	Sales Price	Time Factor	Location Factor	Pool Factor	Adjusted Price
A	Elm	1 Year	$140,000	8% (−$11,200)	0	0	$128,800
B	Elm	1 Month	$130,000	0	0	−$8,000	$122,000
C	Elm	1 Month	$133,000	0	0	0	$133,000
D	Maple	1 Month	$125,000	0	+ $5,000	0	$130,000

similar to two other homes on Elm Street, house B and house C, and another home, house D, on Maple Street (three blocks away). House A sold, one year ago, for $140,000, at a time when the housing market was booming. Houses B, C, and D all sold within the past month. House B sold for $130,000, house C sold for $133,000, and house D sold for $125,500. (Table 6.1)

Example of a time adjustment. A study of the real estate section of the local newspaper, or talks with a real estate agent or with your assessor, indicate that, a year ago, houses were generally selling for about 8 percent higher than they are now.

Because your home is inferior to a comparable home with respect to price (the selling prices of homes has dropped 8 percent in the course of a year), adjust the sale price of this comparable home downward to make it more like your home.

Perform the time adjustment for house A as follows: take 8 percent of the sales price of house A.

$$(\$140,000 \times 0.08 = \$11,200)$$

Next, subtract that amount from the sales price to give you an adjusted price of $128,000.

$$(\$140,000 - \$11,200 = \$128,800)$$

Example of a location adjustment. There is a light industrial park located behind Maple Street. Because of this, homes on Maple Street generally sell for around $5000 less than homes on Elm Street. Because your home is in a better neighborhood, adjust the value of home A upward by $5000 (from $125,500 to $130,500) to make it more like your home.

Example of a physical adjustment. House B on Elm Street has a swimming pool. It is the only comparable home with a pool. You've found that on Elm Street, a pool adds approximately $8000 to the value of the home. Your own home doesn't have a pool. Because your home is inferior to comparable home B, adjust the value of home B downward to $122,000 to make it more like your home.

$$(\$130,000 - \$8000 = \$122,000)$$

Determining the value of adjustments By now, you may be wondering how to figure out what value the marketplace attributes to a particular aspect or feature of a property.

Simply use the same sources of information listed earlier in this chapter to find comparable sales.

For example, ask at the assessor's office what are valid price adjustment for the items you have in mind. If you need to make adjustments to your comparable for time, location, or physical features, the assessor should be able to give you dollar figures for those items.

Real estate agents are also excellent sources for this information. It is in their interests to know exactly how date of sale, location, and physical features affect value.

You can also study homes that are for sale in your area, and try to determine what factors contribute to the asking price of these homes.

The comparable sales form   Now that you understand the concept of making adjustments, and you know where to find the necessary information, you can perform an actual market-data approach.

The instrument that you will use is the comparable sales form shown in Fig. 6.1. You will use this form to list information about, and make adjustments to three comparable sales (Properties A, B, and C), so that you can determine a fair market value for your home.

The first box on the form contains lines for your name and any other owner's name, the address of your property, and the subject map and parcel number that the assessor uses to identify your home.

The second, and larger box, contains four columns and sixteen rows. The first column lists sixteen items that you can (if appropriate) use to determine adjusted sales prices for the three comparable sales (Properties A, B, and C) in each of the remaining columns.

Each of the items has a + or − sign to indicate that you will adjust the value of the comparable up or down.

As mentioned, if your home is better than a comparable home with respect to an item, adjust the sale price of the comparable home upward. If your home is inferior to a comparable home with respect to an item, adjust the sale price of the comparable home downward.

In the residential sales analysis that follows, we'll go through each of the sixteen lines as we compare the comparable homes to the subject home. Then we will determine a final value for the subject.

A residential market analysis   We'll look at the Comparable Sales Form in the following example and learn how to use the market data approach to determine the market value of a home.

Let's pretend that you, the owner of the subject home, have just received notice of the proposed tax bill. The assessor values your property at $165,000. The tax rate of $18.50 per thousand dollars of assessed value results in a total of $3052 (rounded), which you owe. However, you believe the assessed value is too high. To prove it, you select three homes to compare with your own. (We are using three homes to simplify the example. You should use a minimum of five homes.)

In the example, the property rights conveyed are fee simple, the financing is typical, and the conditions of sale for the three comparable homes are all at "arm's length." (Remember to select comparable properties that need no adjustments for financing, sale conditions, or property rights conveyed.)

We also assume that the following conditions exist in our hypothetical real estate market: property values have risen 3 percent per year during the past year. Land is valued at $40,000 per acre (or $0.92/\text{ft}^2$).

The subject home and three comparable homes are described as follows:

The subject home is a 5-year-old colonial, with cedar shingles, on Harbor Road. It has a two-car garage, full finished basement, one and a half bathrooms, four bedrooms, a dining room, living room, and kitchen. The total living area is 1900

FORM #4: COMPARABLE SALES

(NOTE: Unless otherwise noted, sales reflect all property rights, normal financing terms and arm's length transactions. For all other factors, make + or – dollar value adjustments in each row as appropriate.)

OWNER NAME(S):	John Smith
SUBJECT PROPERTY ADDRESS:	1 Harbor Road
SUBJECT MAP AND PARCEL NUMBER:	120-021

	COMPARABLE A		COMPARABLE B		COMPARABLE C	
1. Property Address	7 Harbor Rd		10 Ash St.		3 Bayview Dr.	
2. Sale Price	$135,000		$120,000		$145,000	
3. Date of Sale / + or –	2 mo.		1 yr.		1 mo.	
4. Location / + or –	similar		worse		similar	
5. Home SQ/FT Size / + or –	1,900 sq ft		1,800 sq ft	+6,388	1,850 sq ft	+4,189
6. Number of Rooms / + or –	7		7		8	-9,000
7. Number of Baths / + or –	1½		2½	-4,000	2	-2,000
8. Garage / + or –	2 car		1 car	+6,000	2 car	
9. Pool / + or –	No		No		No	
10. Deck or Porch / + or –	No	+4,000	No	+4,000	No	+4,000
11. Basement / + or –	Full finished		Full finished		Full finished	
12. Fireplace / + or –	1		1		1	
13. Other Features / + or –					Florida room	-8,000
14. Age / + or –	5 yrs.		12 yrs.	+8,050	4 yrs.	
15. Condition / + or –	Very good		Fair	+6,000	Good	
16. Land / + or –	15,000 sq ft		10,800 sq ft	+3,864	13,000 sq ft	+1,840
FINAL ADJUSTED SALES PRICE	$139,000		$158,902		$136,029	

Figure 6.1. Comparable sales form.

ft^2, and the lot size is 100 ft × 150 ft. It also has a fireplace and a redwood deck. The quality of construction is very good. Landscaping is above average. It was purchased four years ago.

Comparable A is a 5-year-old colonial, located nearby on Harbor Road. Its exterior walls are covered with cedar shingles. It has a two-car garage, full finished basement, one and a half bathrooms, four bedrooms, a dining room, living room, and kitchen. The total living area is 1900 ft^2, and the lot size is 100 ft × 150 ft. It has a fireplace, the quality of construction is very good, and the landscaping is average. This home was purchased by its present owner two months ago for $135,000.

Comparable B is a twelve-year-old colonial located on Ash Street, in a less desirable neighborhood. Its exterior walls are covered with cedar shingles. It has a one-car garage, full finished basement, two and a half bathrooms, four bedrooms, a dining room, living room, and kitchen. The total living area is 1800 ft^2, and the lot size is 120 ft × 90 ft. It has a fireplace, the quality of construction is fair, and the landscaping is average. This home was purchased by its present owner one year ago for $120,000.

Comparable C is a 4-year-old colonial, located on Bayview Drive, in a neighborhood similar to the subject. Its exterior walls are covered with cedar shingles. It has a two-car garage, full basement, two bathrooms, four bedrooms, a dining room, living room, library, and kitchen. The total living area is 1850 ft^2, and the lot size is 100 ft × 130 ft. It has a fireplace and a Florida room, the quality of construction is good, and the landscaping is average. This home was purchased by its present owner one month ago for $145,000. (See Fig. 6.1)

With this information, let's look at each line of the comparable sales form.

Line 1: Property address   In this line, we've put the street address of each of the comparable homes.

Line 2: Sale price   In this line, we've placed the sale price of each comparable home.

Line 3: Date of sale   Since property values have risen steadily, averaging 3 percent per year in this area, an adjustment must be made to reflect the change in value over time.

Because comparable properties A and C sold recently (one and two months earlier), no adjustments are necessary.

Comparable B sold one year ago. Its value would have risen 3 percent, or $3600 in that time ($120,000 × 0.03 = $3600). Because the subject home is superior to the comparable (prices are higher now than they were one year ago), we have to adjust the sales price of comparable B upward by $3600 to make it more similar to the subject. We put a + in front of the $3600 and place it as shown in line 3 of the property B column.

A 3 percent per year increase is significant. If our hypothetical market was flat, with little increase or decrease in value over several years, no adjustment for the date of sale would be necessary.

Line 4: Location   Comparable property A is located in the same neighborhood as the subject property. No adjustment is necessary.

Comparable B has a less desireable location. We've found out from a local real estate agent that this location decreases value by $5000. Because the subject home is superior to comparable B with respect to location, we adjust the sales price of comparable home B upward by $5000 to make it more similar to the subject. We put a + in front of the $5000 and place it, as shown, in line 4 of the property B column.

Comparable C is in a similar location. No adjustment is necessary.

Line 5: Home square foot size   Total living square-foot area is a physical feature that is important to most buyers. Dividing the sales price of the home by the total square-foot area gives the value of the home per square foot.

Comparable A has 1900 ft^2. This is similar to the subject. No adjustment is necessary.

Comparable B has 1800 ft^2. This is 100 less ft^2 than the subject. In this case, $115,000 divided by 1800 ft^2 yields a value of $63.88/$ft^2$. Multiplying $63.88 by the 100 ft^2 yields an extra $6388 in value.

Because the subject home is superior to comparable B with respect to square-foot area, we adjust the sales price of comparable B up by $6388 to make it more similar to the subject. We put a + in front of $6388 and place it, as shown, in line 5 for comparable property B.

Comparable C has 1850 ft^2. This is 50 less ft^2 than the subject. In this case, $155,000 divided by 1850 ft^2 yields a value of $83.78/$ft^2$. Multiplying $83.78 by the 50 ft^2 yields an extra $4189 in value.

Because the subject home is superior to comparable C with respect to square-foot area, we adjust the sales price of comparable C up by $4189 to make it more similar to the subject. We put a + in front of the $4189 and place it, as shown, in line 5 for comparable property C.

Line 6: Number of rooms   We've learned from our real estate agent friend that each additional room adds approximately $9000 in value to a home.

Comparable homes A and B each have seven rooms. This is the same as the subject. There is no need to make any adjustment.

Comparable C has eight rooms. This is one more room than the subject.

Because the subject home is inferior to comparable C with respect to the number of rooms, we adjust the sales price of comparable C down by $9000 to make it more similar to the subject. We put a − in front of the $9000 and place it, as shown, in line 6 for comparable property C.

Line 7: Number of baths   We've learned from our real estate agent friend that each additional bathroom adds approximately $4000 in value to a home.

Comparable A has one and a half bathrooms. This is the same as the subject. There is no need to make any adjustment.

Comparable B has two and a half bathrooms. This is one more than the subject.

Because the subject home is inferior to comparable B with respect to the number of bathrooms, we adjust the sales price of comparable B down by $4000 to make it more similar to the subject. We put a − in front of the $4000 and place it, as shown, in line 7 for comparable property B.

Comparable C has two bathrooms. The subject has one and a half bathrooms.

Because the subject home is inferior to comparable C with respect to the number of bathrooms, we adjust the sales price of comparable C down by $2000 to make it more similar to the subject. We put a − in front of the $2000 and place it, as shown, in line 7 for comparable property C.

Line 8: Garage   Each bay of a garage adds about $12,000 to the value of a home.

Comparable homes A and C each have a two-car garage. This is the same as the subject. There is no need to make any adjustment.

Comparable B has a one-car garage. This is one bay less than the subject.

Because the subject home is superior to comparable B with respect to garage size, we adjust the sales price of comparable B up by $6000 to make it more similar to the subject. We put a + in front of the $6000 and place it, as shown, in line 8 for comparable property B.

Line 9: Pool   There is no pool in either the subject or the comparable sales. We enter nothing here.

Line 10: Deck or porch   A redwood deck adds approximately $4000 to the value of a home.

Because the subject home is superior to comparable A, B, and C with respect to this feature, we adjust the sales price of each of the comparable homes up by $4000 to make each more similar to the subject. We put a + in front of the $4000 and place it, as shown, in line 10 for each of the comparable homes.

Line 11: Basement   Because each home has a full basement, there are no adjustments necessary here.

Line 12: Fireplace   Because each home has a fireplace, no adjustments are necessary here.

Line 13: Other features   A Florida room adds approximately $8000 to the value of a home.

Because the subject home is inferior to comparable C with respect to the Florida room, we adjust the sales price of comparable C down by $8000 to make it more similar to the subject. We put a −$8000 in line 13 for comparable property C.

Line 14: Age   The age of a home, measured as depreciation, has an affect on value. There are several methods of determining depreciation (see Chap. 6). We've questioned our assessor and found that the type of homes we are using as comparable homes depreciate at a rate of about 1 percent a year.

Comparable A is the same age as the subject. No adjustment is necessary.

Comparable B is seven years older than the subject. Multiplying the depreciation rate of 1 percent by seven years yields a depreciation of 7 percent. Multiplying the sales price by 7 percent produces the depreciation of comparable B in relation to the subject home. (0.07 × $115,000 = $8050)

Because the subject home is superior to comparable B with respect to age, we adjust the sales price of comparable home B upward by $8050 to make it more similar to the subject. We put a + in front of the $8050 and place it, as shown, in line 14 of the property B column.

Comparable C is one year younger than the subject. Because it is close to the subject in age, no adjustment is necessary.

Line 15: Condition The condition of a home has an affect on value. Condition may relate to construction or maintenance.

The quality of construction of comparable homes A and C are similar to the subject. There is no need to make any adjustment.

The construction of comparable B is fair. We find out from our real estate agent friend that a house of this quality of construction generally sells for about $6000 less than homes constructed like comparable homes A and C, and the subject home.

Because the subject home is superior to comparable B with respect to condition, we adjust the sales price of comparable B up by $6000 to make it more similar to the subject. We put a + in front of the $6000 and place it, as shown, in line 15 for comparable property B.

The landscaping of the subject home is superior to each of the comparable properties. But while it is nicer, our real estate agent tells us that it would not add much to a selling price. There is no need to make any adjustment.

Line 16: Lot ft² size Lot size is compensated for in the same manner that home square-foot size was adjusted above. Land, in our hypothetical situation, is valued at $0.92/ft².

Comparable A has a lot size of 15,000 (100 ft × 150 ft). This is the same as the subject. There is no need to make any adjustment.

Comparable B has a lot size of 10,800 (120 ft − 90 ft). This is 4200 ft² less than the subject. In this case, 4200 ft² multiplied by $0.92 yields a value of $3864.

Because the subject home is superior to comparable B with respect to lot size, we adjust the sales price of comparable B up by $3864 to make it more similar to the subject. We put a + in front of the $3864 and place it, as shown, in line 16 for comparable property B.

Comparable C has a lot size of 13,000 ft² (100 ft − 130 ft). This is 2000 less ft² than the subject. In this case, 2000 multiplied by $0.92 yields a value of $1840.

Because the subject home is superior to comparable C with respect to lot size, we adjust the sales price of comparable C up by $1840 to make it more similar to the subject. We put a + in front of the $1840 and place it, as shown, in line 16 for comparable property C.

Step 3: Reconciling the differences and determining value. At this point, we determine the adjusted sales price of each comparable by adding or subtracting the adjusted amounts, as appropriate, in each column.

You might think that now you simply add each of the adjusted sales prices together and get an average price. Rather than simply average the values, however, a more valid approach is to weigh, more heavily, those comparable properties that are most similar to the subject home.

One way to determine which comparable houses are most similar is to see which require the least adjustments. (Remember, we recommend using a minimum of five comparable properties. We've used three to simplify our example.)

In our example, comparable A is most similar to the subject. It is in the same neighborhood and seems to be a very close physical match to the subject home. It is also a recent sale. Because it is the most similar, we'll place more emphasis on this comparable.

Comparable property B requires the greatest number of adjustments. It is an older sale and the comparable least similar to the subject. Because of these factors, we won't place too much emphasis on this comparable.

Comparable C is a good comparable. While it is a larger home, it is similar to the subject as far as location, age, and condition. It is also a recent sale. Because of this, we will consider this comparable in reaching our conclusion.

After studying our comparable homes, it becomes apparent to us that the value of the subject home should be somewhere between comparable properties A ($139,000) and C ($136,029). Because comparable A needed the least adjustments, we decide the adjusted price of the subject home is nearer to comparable A than it is to comparable C. We decide on a value for the subject home of $138,500.

Let's see what the result would be if we simply averaged the adjusted sales prices of all three comparable homes:

Comparable A	Adjusted Selling Price	$139,000
Comparable B	Adjusted Selling Price	$158,902
Comparable C	Adjusted Selling Price	+ $136,029
		$433,931

$433,931 ÷ 3 = $144,643

The resulting average adjusted selling price of $144,643 is $6143 higher than if we had weighted the results in favor of the closer comparables.

Of course, we could just as easily conclude that the subject is worth $138,000 or $137,500. These are subjective estimates that are based on our market data. Subjective estimates that are, as the saying goes, in the ballpark.

The point to appreciate here is that different individuals using the same data could arrive at different conclusions of value. But chances are that with the same data, the differences would not be great.

Some important points to remember are:

1. If you choose very similar comparable properties, it will be easier to determine the value of the subject home and easier to defend your conclusion.

2. The more comparable homes that you use, the easier it is to arrive at a conclusion.

3. By weighting the results in favor of those comparables most like your home, your final opinion of value will be more valid than if you simply average the price of each.

In our example, we have determined that the value of the subject home is $138,500. This is $26,500 less than the assessor's $165,000 value determination. At a tax rate of $18.50 per thousand dollars of value, this would result in a tax bill of $2,562.25.

$$(\$18.50 \times 138.5 = \$2,562.25)$$

This is $489.75 less than the original bill of $3052. If this error was carried for five years between revaluations, the owner would pay an extra $2,448.75 in property taxes. Taxes which could have been avoided. And, of course, if the tax rate increased each year, the amount overpaid could be much greater.

Summary

The market-data approach measures the actions of buyers and sellers in the marketplace, using data taken directly from the marketplace.

Certain elements are always considered in the market-data approach. These are:

1. The property rights conveyed
2. Financing terms
3. Conditions of the sale
4. The location of a property
5. The date of sale
6. Physical features of a property

Basic steps in the market data approach are:

1. The location of recently sold comparative properties.
2. The comparison of the comparative properties to the subject property through the adjustment process.
3. The reconciliation of differences between the comparative properties and the subject, and the determination of a market value for the subject.

Property Tax Exemptions

The calm confidence of a Christian with four aces.

MARK TWAIN

You can have that kind of confidence when your property-tax bill comes around, if you qualify for an exemption or two.

What Are Exemptions?

An exemption excuses you from paying all, or part of your property tax. It is the easiest way to save on your property-tax bill, and it involves none of the work that other chapters of this book require of you. All you have to do is find out what exemptions are available in your area, and then apply for those for which you qualify.

Property-tax exemptions have historically been given to religious, educational, and charitable organizations in the belief that such exemptions promote the general welfare.

Over time, the scope of ideas for promoting the general welfare has increased. And so has the range of exemptions. For example, a company may receive a property-tax exemption if it builds a plant or office building. The exemption is granted in the belief that the plant or office building contributes to the general welfare by creating jobs. This idea has been extended to all kinds of properties, including golf courses, airports, theaters, and apartment buildings.

Today, almost one-third of all property in this country is exempt from property taxes, either completely or partially. Exemptions apply chiefly to the following types of property:

- Property owned by the federal government
- State owned property
- Property owned by local government
- Property owned by religious, charitable, or service groups
- Industrial and commercial property identified as serving the public good
- Residential property

Religious use properties are exempt because the United States Constitution prohibits government's interference with the practice of religion. The same document also contains the legal basis that prevents states from taxing federal properties.

We'll look at some exemptions that are available to residential property owners.

Individual state constitutions usually are the source of a state's right to grant exemptions. State legislatures make laws allowing particular kinds of exemptions based on this constitutional power. Municipalities then apply these laws at the local level.

Available exemptions are different in each state. And within each state, local taxing jurisdictions (county, town, city, village, or school district) may have the option of allowing or disallowing particular exemptions.

For example, a state may allow some form of partial property-tax exemption for volunteer fire fighters. A particular fire fighter may live in an area where the county, town, village, and school district all allow the exemption. In that case, the full value of the exemption is available to the fire fighter. But, if the fire fighter lives in an area where only the village allows the exemption, then the fire fighter must pay the full tax to the county, town, and school district.

Exempt property means lost revenue to local taxing jurisdictions. Revenue that has to be made up in some other way. This usually means that the tax rate increases so that those properties that are taxed can satisfy budget needs. Some municipalities contain a high percentage of exempt properties and are stuck with a narrow tax base and high tax rates.

Most states provide assessors with guidelines concerning the types of owners and the types of properties that may qualify for exemptions. It is up to the assessor to interpret the guidelines and apply the exemptions fairly.

Normally, guidelines direct that certain eligibility standards be satisfied to obtain the exemption. These requirements differ from state to state. And within a state, the requirements differ from one taxing jurisdiction to another.

In one area, for example, anyone who owns a particular type of property may apply for an appropriate exemption. Other areas may have more rigorous eligibility requirements.

Eligibility requirements are, for the most part, about ownership, location, use, and time.

Ownership requirements may refer to the owner's occupation (e.g., clergy or fireman). They may refer to the owner's status as a veteran or a disabled person. Or they can refer to the owner's age or income.

Location requirements may direct that the property be located in a certain type of area (e.g., low-income areas, flood areas, urban neighborhoods).

Use requirements examine the way that the property is used. The property may have to be occupied by its owner, or it may have to be used as a residence only. It may have to be occupied by a family within certain income limits, or it may have to be used for specific business purposes. An exemption based on use may require the fulfillment of one condition, or several conditions, in order to qualify.

Time requirements demand that a condition be completed by a particular date.

For example, a solar heater must be installed or an owner must take possession by a certain date. If either act occurred past the qualifying date, no exemption is possible.

Common exemptions

The following paragraphs contain a list of common exemptions. These will vary from state to state. If your state provides for exemptions, check with your assessor to see if local taxing jurisdictions allow the exemptions.

Blind/disabled: Physically disabled or blind homeowners may be eligible for certain exemptions. To qualify, it may be necessary that a blind or physically disabled person own the home, or it may only be necessary that a blind or physically disabled person be a member of the household. In almost all cases, the impairment must be permanent and certified by a physician.

Disabled or deceased police or fire fighters: Some areas offer exemptions to the spouse or children of deceased or disabled police or fire fighters.

Environmental exemptions: Certain exemptions are provided for homes that use solar or wind powered energy devices, or other antipollution equipment.

Farm or agricultural exemptions: This provides exemptions for property used for agricultural purposes. It protects the farmer or rancher with property in a fast growing area. As the area grows, land becomes more valuable and property assessments increase. The farm or agricultural exemption allows the property's assessment to be based on its value as a farm or ranch.

Historical property: Certain properties that are formally declared of historic interest may be eligible for tax exemptions.

Hardship cases: Homeowner's who have come on hard times may find that they are eligible for exemptions.

Home business: Certain areas offer exemptions to homeowners who operate businesses from their homes.

Homestead exemption: This exempts a portion of the assessed value of your home from the property tax. For example, in Florida, a homeowner may file for a $25,000 homestead tax exemption. On a home whose value is assessed at $100,000, this exemption means that the owner pays taxes on $75,000. A significant savings. Check with your assessor for the requirements in your area. This is, perhaps, the most common exemption available to homeowners.

Household items: In areas that tax personal property, certain necessary household items (e.g., refrigerator, range, furniture, and other common household goods) may be exempt.

Low-income household: An exemption may be allowed if your income is below a particular level. The tax may be held at a certain level by a circuit breaker feature (a feature which protects elderly people on a fixed-income from ruinous property-tax increases).

Mobile homes: Mobile homes may be eligible for exemptions even if they are located on another's property.

Orphaned minors: Some areas provide exemptions for property owned by orphaned minors.

Religious exemption: Exemptions generally apply to houses of worship; however, in some areas a minister's (or spouse's) residence may be eligible for an exemption. This exemption may apply to a religious person no longer able to perform religious work because of age or impairment.

Senior citizen: This exemption is usually restricted to homeowners over 65 years of age, although the age limit can vary. There may be other specific requirements, such as the property must be the homeowner's permanent residence. You may have to provide proof of age. You may have to prove how long you owned the property, or prove that the property is only used for residential purposes. If you are in a nursing home, but still own the home, you may still be eligible. The exemption usually provides for a partial exemption from payment of property taxes.

In some areas, there is a provision that makes it possible for senior citizens to keep their homes even if they don't have the money to pay their property taxes. Typically, it allows banks to provide loans for past, present, or future property-tax bills. The loans may be secured by a first or second mortgage, and the principal amount can be adjusted to compensate for additional taxes. Such a loan is not due until the property is sold or disposed of. It may be paid off at any time.

Circuit breaker for the elderly: This protects elderly people on a fixed income from ruinous property tax increases. When the tax reaches a certain percentage of the homeowner's income, the breaker kicks in to hold the tax at that level.

Veteran: Exemptions generally apply to veterans, or if the veteran is deceased, to a surviving, unmarried spouse or child, if the property is a primary residence. Exemptions may be based on different circumstances including war time status, combat zone activity, or disability.

Widows exemption: Widows may be eligible for exemptions. These exemptions may apply to widows of veterans, police, fire fighters, or widows in general.

What Is Available?

You can find out what exemptions are available in your area by asking your assessor. Ask for a list of exemptions, qualifying requirements, deadlines for filing, and applications.

The list of exemptions specifies what exemptions are available in your area. Be sure to ask your assessor to explain any eligibility requirements that are not clear to you.

Be certain that you understand what the qualifying requirements are. You may be eligible, but you won't receive the exemption unless you provide exactly what is required. The assessing office may require that you submit both an application form and proof of eligibility for particular exemptions.

If you find that you are eligible for an exemption, you must file the appropriate forms at the time that the law requires. If you don't, you won't receive the exemption. There are usually no allowances for extenuating circumstances. Remember, it's up to you to find out what forms are necessary, and when they must be submitted to the assessor.

When exploring an exemption, check to see:

1. What owners and property types are eligible?
2. Which taxing jurisdictions allow the exemption?
3. Is the property wholly or partially exempt?
4. Is the exemption mandatory or optional for each taxing jurisdiction?

Calculating Your Exemption

Your exemption may be a fixed dollar amount or a percentage of the total assessed value of your property. In either case, it is easily calculated.

If it is a fixed dollar amount (like the $25,000 homestead exemption in Florida), simply subtract the amount of the exemption from the assessed value of your home.

If the exemption is a percentage of your assessed value, multiply your home's total assessed value by the percentage. Then subtract the result from the total assessed value.

Calculations get more complex if you are eligible for more that one exemption. Certain tax districts allow you the full amount of each of your exemptions. Other districts impose a limit on multiple exemptions. Again, check with your assessor.

If you have applied for, and received an exemption, your assessor will have performed the appropriate calculations.

Summary

Exemptions usually promote the common good. Exemptions vary from state to state, and from one locale to another within a state. Assessors interpret state guidelines concerning exemptions to determine eligibility. Eligibility requirements concern questions of ownership, location, use, and time. In applying for an exemption, the applicant must meet all requirements, using the proper forms, at the appropriate deadline.

8

Organizing Your Tax Appeal

You may have to fight a battle more than once to win it.
                    MARGARET THATCHER (b. 1925),
                         British prime minister

This chapter describes how to organize and present your case for a lower property-assessment or property tax abatement. It includes examples of an appeal of both a single family home and a condominium unit.

The word *appeal* refers to any taxpayer request for a review of a property-tax assessment, regardless of the form it takes. It may be an informal meeting with the assessor or a full blown presentation before a board of review, but it will still involve similar steps. You should, however, be aware of the difference between a tax abatement versus a permanent change to a property's assessed value.

A *tax abatement* is a refund of taxes due a taxpayer, regardless of the reason for the overpayment. Award of a tax abatement does not necessarily result in a permanent change to the assessed value of a property. The refund of taxes paid may indicate only a temporary value adjustment by the assessor, often just for the tax year in question. For example, the assessor may recognize a short-term change in housing market demand and grant an abatement of taxes paid for a particular year.

When a permanent change to a property's *assessed value* occurs, the value change will be effective until the next district wide revaluation of all properties. Revaluation periods typically vary from one year to a decade or longer. Assessed value changes can affect the taxes assessed on a property for many years. Assessment changes may even, in some cases, be applied retroactively to previous tax years, although this is less common.

Of course, it is preferable for a lower assessment to be applied for more than one tax year. However, since some jurisdictions only make permanent assessment changes during revaluation years, it may not be possible to do so. If you are awarded a tax abatement, you may have to reapply for a similar abatement each year until a revaluation of all properties has taken place. Check with your local assessor to determine when permanent changes to assessed property values are made as the result of tax appeals.

Main Steps in Organizing Your Appeal

The main steps required in nearly all appeals are similar, and are summarized below. Appendix B contains forms designed to help you collect much of the information described below in an orderly fashion. The forms are referenced following each step listed.

Step 1: Gather information about the assessor's office and appeal procedures

- What are the important tax calendar dates?
- What assessor records are available for you to review? (Property record cards, cost manuals, assessing manuals, etc.)
- What constitute legal assessing errors?
- What are the various stages of appeal available, and when may I appeal?
- Are informal meetings with the assessor to resolve the dispute possible? When?
- What exemptions am I eligible for?
- When is the next scheduled revaluation of district properties?
- What help is available to me, such as copies of informational pamphlets, state assessing manuals, or informational property tax seminars? Are there any taxpayer associations operating in my area that could offer guidance?

(See "Form #1: Assessor's Office Checklist," Appendix B, for more detail.)

Step 2: Gather information about your own and comparable properties. Secure copies of:

- Property deed
- Property record card
- Photographs of property
- Current and last tax bill
- Master plan (if condominium)
- Professional appraisal if available and recent
- Cost approach data, either from a commercial cost manual or from the assessor's cost manual or other source.
- Records of comparable property sales to use in comparable sales approach to value.

(See "Form #2: Tax Appeal Checklist," Appendix B, for more detail.)

Step 3: Review assessor's opinion of value for your property.

- Convert assessed value to fair market value if assessed value is less than 100 percent of fair market value.

- Look for errors in the three main categories:
  1. Mechanical errors (descriptive, mathematical, or clerical errors.)
  2. General assessment errors (for example, property assessed at more than fair market value.)
  3. Legal errors
- Document any assessing errors you feel exist and note items to discuss and clarify with assessor if not clear from records.
- Review sales assessment ratio study and equalization study for your area if available. Use to compare the assessed value of your property with other properties in its class.

(See "Form #3: Checklist of Assessing Errors," Appendix B, for more detail.)

Step 4: Prepare your own opinion of value for your property.

- Utilize comparable sales approach to value. (Use "Form #4: Comparable Sales Form," Appendix B, or similar form.)
- Utilize cost approach to value. (Use "Form #5: Cost Approach Worksheet," Appendix B, or similar form.)
- Utilize professional appraisal if available and recent. (It is not necessary to do so, but if a professionally prepared appraisal is available, it will save you some time and effort. It will already include a cost approach and a comparable sales approach to value for your home.)
- Consider all exemptions to which you may be entitled.
- Gather other supporting evidence, such as statements of experts, relative to the property's value.

Step 5: Present your findings to the assessor.

- Utilize any required municipal forms, adhere to deadlines for filing.
- Summarize your main points in a one-page cover letter. Be certain it includes a statement of your opinion of value for the property.
- Include copies of all evidence and supporting material.
- Be sure to get a date-stamped receipt proving timely submission of your application and evidence.
- If the appeal is resolved to your satisfaction in an informal meeting with the assessor, ask for a written copy of the decision, before the deadline to submit a formal appeal has expired.

(See "Form #2: Tax Appeal Checklist," Appendix B, for more.)

Sample Appeal Cases

The two sample appeal cases that follow, show how you might organize your own appeal. Each contains a brief summary of facts to help you see what the issues are and what arguments the taxpayers raised. Following each fact summary is the completed tax appeal containing everything that the taxpayers submitted to the assessor. While every case is a little different, these should give you an idea of what a typical, well organized appeal looks like in finished form. The outcome of each appeal has been left intentionally undecided. Decide for yourself if each property owner has a valid case.

Just as with your own appeal, you will need to take time to look carefully at the property record cards and other information to see just what the errors are. A calculator will be helpful.

Ask questions as you go through the examples. Are the taxpayers challenging specific aspects of the assessment? Do they offer alternatives to the assessor? What kinds of errors have they uncovered? Can you draw similarities between the examples and your own property?

The first appeal involves a single family house, while the second deals with a condominium. Both properties are located in a fictitious New Hampshire town called Hamptonshire, in the make believe county of Rockingstone.

As general background on both cases, the town of Hamptonshire has just conducted a revaluation of all properties, the first such revaluation in five years. The town has announced that it intends to assess all properties at 100 percent of market value. Having just received notice of the new assessment for their properties, the owners of both properties have filed abatement applications in which they dispute the assessments.

Case 1: Single Family House

Summary of facts

The owner, Constance Weld, purchased her home three years ago for $125,000. It is a 1800 ft^2, ranch-style house built on a parcel of land measuring 30,000 ft^2 in size. The house is 15-years-old and is in good condition. It has been generally well maintained, experiencing normal wear and tear for its age.

The house has three bedrooms, a family room, dining room, full kitchen, a full finished basement, and one and a half bathrooms. It also has a two-car garage, a screened-in porch, and a small deck.

It is located in a good neighborhood that is made up of homes of similar size and age. A number of similar homes in the neighborhood have sold in the past six months.

Based on the results of the revaluation in Hamptonshire, Constance's home has been assessed at $159,750 (land $39,800, building $119,950). Previously the property was assessed at $106,000 (land $25,000, building $81,000).

After a review of the assessor's property record card and other property information, Constance feels that assessment errors have occurred. She has prepared a written appeal to present to the town assessor. The items contained in the appeal are:

1. A cover letter stating her opinion of value and summarizing the main reasons she feels the property is too highly assessed.
2. A more detailed explanation of her reasons for seeking the abatement.
3. Photographs of the subject property and comparable properties
4. A completed comparable sales approach to value for the subject property
5. A completed cost approach to value for the subject property
6. A sales assessment ratio study summary
7. An equalization study summary
8. A copy of the property deed
9. The required town property-tax abatement application form

See Case 1, Exhibits A–K on pages 94–104.

Text continues on page 105.

                                              15 Woods End Lane
                                              Hamptonshire, NH

Town of Hamptonshire Assessor
Town Hall
123 Main Street
Hamptonshire, NH

Dear Sir:

   Enclosed is an Application for Abatement of Taxes on the
property located at 15 Woods End Lane, Hamptonshire, Map/lot No.
345-015-000. I believe the assessed value of $159,750 (land
$39,800, building $119,950) to be in error. For the following
reasons I feel a more accurate assessed value is $123,800.

1.   A land measurement error as recorded on the property record
card incorrectly lists the land size as "39,000 sq. ft." when the
actual size is 30,000 sq.ft as shown on the deed for the property
(copy enclosed).

2.   A comparable sales approach to value indicates a full market
value for this property of $133,000. (Enclosed)

3.   A cost approach to value using cost data supplied by your
office indicates a full replacement value for this property of
$131,590. (Enclosed)

4.   The property record card contains the following descriptive
errors of my property:
     a. two fireplaces listed when there is only one
     b. unheated, screened in porch is listed as 150 sq. ft. of
living area
     c. an extra half bath is listed
     d. an insufficient amount of depreciation is allowed

5.   A sales/assessment ratio analysis of other neighborhood
homes and Rockingston County's recent equalization study indicate
that most properties in Hamptonshire are not yet assessed at 100%
of full market value. Assessing my property at a greater rate
than other residential properties in Hamptonshire is not fair and
equitable.

   I have attached a more detailed explanation supporting these
points.

   Your attention to this matter is appreciated.

Sincerely,

Constance Weld

Constance Weld

CASE 1. EXHIBIT A.

Further Explanation

1. Land Value - The property record card lists 9,000 more square feet of land than I actually own, as shown on the attached copy of my property deed. Accepting the land value of $1.02 per square foot used by the assessor's office, this has resulted in an assessment error of $9,200. The full market value of my parcel is therefore $30,600. (30,000 × $1.02 = $30,600)

2. Comparable Sales Approach - The attached worksheet and photographs indicates that three recent sales of very similar homes in close proximity to my own show a reasonable value for my home of $133,000.

3. Cost Approach - The attached cost approach worksheet, using square foot costs and multipliers from the Hamptonshire Assessor's cost manual, indicates a replacement value of $100,990 for my home, not including the land value of $30,600. I have used a depreciation amount of 10%. For my 15 year old home in good condition it is the suggested amount from the cost manual, rather than the 5% figure shown on the property record card.

Also, I have noted several errors on the property record card.

First, the living area of my home measures 60' × 30', or 1,800 sq. ft. rather than 62' × 32', or 1,984 sq. ft. as shown. Also the 150 sq. ft. porch should not be included in the total living area of the home. The correct total living area is 1,800 sq. ft., rather than 2,134 sq. ft. as shown on the property record card.

Secondly, I have included the cost of one fireplace, rather than two as noted on the record card.

The resulting replacement value, including land and depreciation for my home is more accurately figured at $131,590. Since this is quite close to the figure of $133,000 which I arrived at using the comparable sales approach, I believe the fair market value for my property should be $133,000.

The Town of Hamptonshire does not yet assess all properties at 100% of fair market value. I have attached my own sales/assessment ratio worksheet showing that the average assessed value of neighboring properties is about 90% of fair market value. The latest Rockingstone County Equalization Study shows that Hamptonshire assesses residential properties at 93% of fair market value. Since these figures are close, I have used 93% of fair market value to calculate the assessment on my property.

Since most properties are assessed at only about 93% of fair value rather than 100%, it is inequitable to assess my property at 100%. Therefore, a fair assessed value for my property would be 93% of $133,000, or $123,700.

CASE 1. EXHIBIT B.

Town of Hamptonshire

Application for Abatement of Taxes

Date Filed _____ 10-15-92 _____ Tax Year _1992-93_

Name of
Applicant(s) _____ Constance Weld _____

_____

Property
Address _____ 15 Woods End Lane _____

Map - Lot Number _____ 345-015-000 _____

Assessment _____ $159,750 _____

Reasons for filing abatment application:

Property is over assessed. See attached
letter and other supporting evidence.

Signature of Applicant(s) _Constance Weld_____

_____

Mailing Address _____ 15 Woods End Lane _____

_____

Note: The filing of this application does not stay the collection of the taxes due. They should be paid as assessed by the due date. Refund will follow if abatement is allowed.

CASE 1. EXHIBIT C.

I, Charles d'Estries

of Exeter,

County of   of Rockingham

State of
        New Hampshire

for consideration paid, grant to   Constance Weld

of
    7 Moriches Road, Moorewood
County of

State of   Rockingstone   ,

        New Hampshire
with WARRANTY COVENANTS,

(Description and incumbrance, if any)

A certain tract or parcel of land, with the buildings thereon, situated in Hamptonshire, County of Rockingstone, being shown as Lot #15 on a Plan of Land in Hamptonshire, New Hampshire showing "Woods End Estates" as subdivided for Alfred Bartow, May 1991, said plan being recorded as Plan No, 23567 in the Rockingstone County Registry of Deeds, and being more particularly bounded and described as follows:

Beginning at the most northerly corner of the premises on the south side of Burn Lane and the boundary between Lots No. 12 and No. 11:

thence South 38° 05' East along the southwesterly side of Burn Lane for a distance of one hundred and fifty (150) feet to an iron pin;

thence turning and running South 51° 42' West along the boundary of lots No. 21 and No.22 a distance of two hundred (200) feet to a stake;

thence turning and running North 38° 05' West along the boundary between Lots No. 24 and No.25 a distance of one hundred fifty (150) feet to a stake;

thence turning and running North 51° 51' East along the boundary between lots No. 7 and No. 8 a distance of two hundred (200) feet to a stake on the south side of Burns Lane and the point of beginning.

Meaning and intending to convey Lot No. 15 as shown on said plan having an area of 30,000 square feet, more or less.

        of said Grantor,

release to said Grantee all rights of ownership and other interest therein.

            WITNESS our hands and seals this *15th*day of *June*, **1989**
            Witness:
..........*Constance Weld*..
..........*Charles d'Estries*..
                        COMMONWEALTH OF MASSACHUSETTS

    Then personally appeared the above named   Charles d'Estries + *Constance Weld*
and acknowledged the foregoing instrument to be *their* voluntary act and deed before me.
            ....*Hector Madison*..............
            Notary Public

CASE 1. EXHIBIT D.

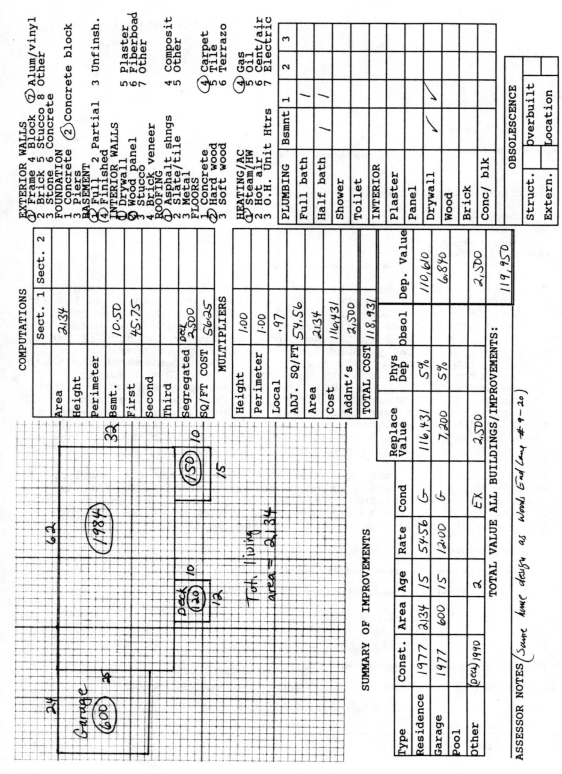

COMPUTATIONS

EXTERIOR WALLS
① Frame 4 Block ⑦ Alum/vinyl
2 Brick 5 Stucco 8 Other
3 Stone 6 Concrete

FOUNDATION
1 Concrete ② Concrete block
3 Piers

BASEMENT
① Full 2 Partial 3 Unfinsh.
④ Finished

INTERIOR WALLS
① Drywall 5 Plaster
2 Wood panel 6 Fiberboad
3 Stucco 7 Other
4 Brick veneer

ROOFING
① Asphalt shngs 4 Composit
2 Slate/tile 5 Other
3 Metal

FLOORS
1 Concrete ④ Carpet
② Hard wood 5 Tile
3 Soft wood 6 Terrazo

HEATING/AC
① Steam/HW ④ Gas
2 Hot air 5 Oil
3 O.H. Unit Htrs 6 Cent/air
7 Electric

	Sect. 1	Sect. 2
Area	2134	
Height		
Perimeter		
Bsmt.	10.50	
First	45.75	
Second		
Third		
Segregated	oct 2,500	
SQ/FT COST	56.25	

MULTIPLIERS

Height	1.00	
Perimeter	1.00	
Local	.97	
ADJ. SQ/FT	54.56	
Area	2134	
Cost	116,431	
Addnt's	2,500	
TOTAL COST	118,931	

PLUMBING	Bsmnt	1	2	3
Full bath		/		
Half bath		/		
Shower				
Toilet				
INTERIOR				
Plaster				
Panel				
Drywall		✓		
Wood				
Brick				
Conc/ blk				

OBSOLESCENCE

Struct.	overbuilt	
Extern.	Location	

SUMMARY OF IMPROVEMENTS

Type	Const.	Area	Age	Rate	Cond	Replace Value	Phys Dep	Obsol	Dep. Value
Residence	1977	2134	15	54.56	G	116,431	5%	5%	110,610
Garage	1977	600	15	12.00	G	7,200	5%		6,840
Pool									
Other	(pool) 1990		2		EX	2,500			2,500

TOTAL VALUE ALL BUILDINGS/IMPROVEMENTS: 119,950

ASSESSOR NOTES (Same home design as Woods End Lane # 9-20)

CASE 1. EXHIBIT E.

98

Parcel #: 345-015-000	RECORD OF OWNERSHIP	DATE	BOOK	PAGE	PRICE	Class	RES
15 Woods End Lane	Charles d'Estries	3-4-77	2334	118	$89,900	Zoning	R1
OWNER: Constance Weld	Constance Weld	6-15-89	3918	325	$125,000	Use	SFR
15 Woods End Lane Hamptonshire, NH						NH Code	RES

ASSESSMENT RECORD

INSPECTION WITNESSED BY:

Visit History	19	19	19	19
D.H. 1977 (8-2-77)				
L.B. 1985 (8-7-85)				

Description	1977	1985	1992	19	19	19	19
Building	65,100	76,000	110,610				
Garage/Non-living	5,900	5,000	6,840				
Other			2,500				
TOTAL VALUE BUILDING	71,000	81,000	119,950				
TOTAL VALUE LAND	18,900	25,000	39,800				
TOTAL LAND & BUILDING	89,900	106,000	159,750				

LAND VALUE COMPUTATIONS AND SUMMARY

Description	Code	Size	Rate	Influence Factor	Land Value
Primary site		39,000	1.02		$39,800
Secondary site					
Undeveloped					
Marshland					
Waterfront					
TOTALS					$39,800

Property Factors		
TOPOGRAPHY	STREET	
Level	✓ Paved	
Hilly	Sidewalk	
Swampy	Unpaved	
NEIGHBORHOOD	IMPROVEMENTS	
✓ Improving	✓ Water	
Static	✓ Electric	
Declining	✓ Sewer	

NOTES: (No visit for 1992 reval — owner not home multiple visits.)

CASE 1. EXHIBIT F.

FORM #4: COMPARABLE SALES

(NOTE: Unless otherwise noted, sales reflect all property rights, normal financing terms and arm's length transactions. For all other factors, make + or − dollar value adjustments in each row as appropriate.)

OWNER NAME(S): Constance Weld

SUBJECT PROPERTY ADDRESS: 15 Woods End Lane

SUBJECT MAP AND PARCEL NUMBER: 345 − 015 − 000

	COMPARABLE A		COMPARABLE B		COMPARABLE C	
1. Property Address	2 Woods End Lane		36 Woods End Lane		7 Burns Lane	
2. Sale Price	$134,500		$128,500		$133,000	
3. Date of Sale / + or −	2 mos.		6 mos.	+1,500	2 mos.	
4. Location / + or −	similar		similar		similar	
5. Home SQ/FT Size / + or −	1,800		1,800		1,800	
6. Number of Rooms / + or −	6		6		6	
7. Number of Baths / + or −	2	−$3,500	1½		1½	
8. Garage / + or −	2 car		2 car		2 car	
9. Pool / + or −	no		no		no	
10. Deck or Porch / + or −	both		both		both	
11. Basement / + or −	full fin.		full unfin.	+$5,000	full fin.	
12. Fireplace / + or −	1		1		1	
13. Other Features / + or −						
14. Age / + or −	15		14		16	
15. Condition / + or −	good		good		good	
16. Land / + or −	30,000		30,000		30,000	
FINAL ADJUSTED SALES PRICE	$131,000		$135,000		$133,000	

CASE 1. EXHIBIT G.

FORM #5: COST APPROACH WORKSHEET

Owner Name(s): *Constance Weld*

Property Address: *15 Woods End Lane*

Property Map & Parcel Number: *345 - 015 - 000*

VALUE OF IMPROVEMENTS

AREA 1: Residence

1. <u>1,800</u> sq/ft × $<u>54.56</u> per sq/ft = $ <u>98,208</u>
   (Living area)   (Cost per sq/ft)   (Cost of living area)

AREA 2: Non-living area (garage, screened porch etc.)

2. <u>750</u> sq/ft × $<u>12.00</u> per sq/ft = $ <u>9,000</u>   (*600 sq.ft.* *150 sq.ft.*
   (Non-living area) (Cost per sq/ft) (Cost of non-living area)   *Garage + porch*)

3. TOTAL of lines 2 and 3: $ <u>107,208</u>

4.   Amounts for extra features:

   Fireplace $ <u>2,500</u>

   Pool $ _____

   Patio $ _____

   Other Special Features (*deck*) $ <u>2,500</u>

5. TOTAL of lines 3 and 4: $ <u>112,208</u>
   (Replacement Cost New)

6. Minus depreciation amount: — $ <u>10 % (or 11,221)</u>

7. Current Value of Improvement $ <u>100,987</u>

VALUE OF LAND

8. Value of Land $ <u>30,600</u>

9. TOTAL value of property
   (line 7 + line 8): $ <u>131,590</u> (*rounded*)

CASE 1. EXHIBIT H.

15 Wood End Lane
Map - Lot # 345-015-000
Owner: Constance Weld

Comparable "A"
2 Woods End Lane
Owner: James Barry

CASE 1.　EXHIBIT I.

Comparable "B"
36 Woods End Lane
Owners: Mark & Jennifer Scurry

Comparable "C"
7 Burn Lane
Owner: Racheal Chilton

CASE 1. EXHIBIT J.

FORM #6: SALES/ASSESSMENT RATIO

DIRECTIONS: Choose 15 to 25 homes that have sold within the past year. Fill in the selling price of each home, as well as the assessed value of each, according to the records in the assessor's office. Divide the assessed value by the selling price of each home to get the assessment rate. Add the total of all the assessment rates (A), then divide by the total number of properties (B) to get the average assessment rate (C). Compare the average assessment rate with the rate that your home has been assessed at.

No.	Street Address	Assessed Value	Divided by	Sales Price	=	Assessment Rate
1	7 Burns La.	123,690	÷	133,000		.93
2	12 Burns LA.	134,425	÷	141,500		.95
3	23 Burns LA.	129,000	÷	142,000		.91
4	36 Woods End	100,000	÷	128,500		.78
5	14 Elm. St.	75,500	÷	99,200		.76
6	1 Oak St.	125,000	÷	139,400		.90
7	20 Apple	189,000	÷	199,500		.95
8	15 Trout La.	67,500	÷	125,000		.54
9	21 Trout LA.	125,000	÷	127,900		.98
10	149 Pine St.	132,700	÷	149,900		.76
11	211 Pine St.	170,000	÷	175,000		.97
12	11 Farm Rd.	275,000	÷	295,700		.93
13	33 Farm Rd.	165,000	÷	192,300		.86
14	18 Town Line Rd	110,500	÷	116,900		.95
15	41 Townline Rd.	110,000	÷	118,500		.93
16	16 Ridgeview	135,900	÷	149,900		.91
17	8 Plum LA.	136,000	÷	136,000		1.00
18	3 Mason St.	115,000	÷	119,500		.96
19	25 Mason St.	120,000	÷	130,000		.92
20	4 Brimstone La	50,000	÷	89,800		.89
21	22 Locust St.	90,000	÷	93,500		.96
22	7 Norton LA.	113,000	÷	118,700		.95
23	15 Wilson Rd	112,500	÷	118,000		.95
24	1 Topper St.	129,900	÷	137,500		.94
25	26 Boynton La	139,900	÷	142,000		.98

A	TOTAL OF ALL ASSESSMENT RATES:	22.56
B	TOTAL NUMBER OF PROPRTIES USED:	25
C	AVERAGE SALES/ASSESSMENT RATIO (LINE "A" DIVIDED BY LINE "B")	.902

CASE 1. EXHIBIT K.

Case 2: Condominium

Because the next case involves a condominium and not a single family home, the owner has an additional factor to consider. He must determine how much of the common area of the condominium development his unit ownership represents. There are always two distinct ownership interests in a condominium. There is the fee-simple ownership of the unit and there is an undivided interest in the common areas. The value of a condominium unit may increase because of changes to the value of common areas or to the unit itself, or to both. If common-area value has increased, all unit values will increase proportionately. An individual unit's assessment should not increase in greater proportion than the percentage of the total development the unit represents. If an individual unit value increases because of custom improvements, common-area value should not increase.

The percentage of common-area ownership may most easily be determined by referring to the property deed or the declaration of condominium, the legal document which formed the condominium. However, if these documents do not contain this information, or if the percentage has changed because new units have been built, there are two ways to determine it.

The two methods are known as the *original price method* and the *area method*. The declaration of condominium usually lists the method used in a condominium development. The area method is most common and is used in the following sample case. Both methods, however, are now described.

Area method of computing common-area ownership

Step 1. Compute the total square-foot living area of all condominiums in the development. If there are multiple styles of units, multiply the number of each type of unit by its living area in square feet, and total.

For example:

Type A: 10 units × 900 ft² = 9000 ft²
Type B: 10 units × 1,200 ft² = 12,000 ft²
Type C: 10 units × 1,350 ft² = 13,500 ft²

Total   34,500 ft²

Step 2. Calculate the percentage of common-area ownership of any type of unit by dividing its square-foot area by the total area of all units in the complex, and multiplying by 100. For example, calculate a B unit's percentage of common area ownership as follows:

$$(1200 \div 34,500) \times 100 = 3.48\%$$

There are two primary sources you may use to determine the total square-foot area of the condominium development. The first is the declaration of condominium, which is a recorded document available at the county courthouse, or wherever documents are recorded in your area. Secondly, the assessor's office will maintain this information, although you may have to look through the property record cards for each unit to find it. Some assessors maintain a summary card describing the total condominium development, and individual cards for each unit. If this is so in your area, the summary card will be a quick means of determining the total area.

Original price method of computing common-area ownership

Step 1. Compute the total original cost of all units.

Type A: 10 units × $85,000 = $850,000
Type B: 10 units × $92,000 = $920,000
Type C: 10 units × $99,000 = $990,000

                         Total $2,760,000

Step 2. Calculate the percentage of common-area ownership of an individual unit by dividing its cost by the total cost of all units combined, and multiplying by 100. For example, calculate a type C unit's percentage of common-area ownership as follows:

$$(\$99,000 \div \$2,760,000) \times 100 = 3.59\%$$

The amount of common-area ownership may or may not be an issue in a property tax appeal. If the assessment on your unit is similar to other units in your condominium complex, it is probably fair *in relation to them*. (It may not be fair in relation to similar condominiums at another development.) If the assessment is very different from similar units at your development, the assessor may have applied the wrong percentage of common-area ownership to your unit.

Summary of facts

Keith McHugh purchased the subject condominium (Unit 211) one year ago for $108,000. It is five-years-old and was purchased from the original owner. It is a two bedroom, one bath unit containing 1840 ft² of living area. Like other B type units in the development, it has a garage and full unfinished basement.

Although the condominium development is five-years-old, some of the buildings have only recently been completed. Newer units include a number of custom interior options that were not available when Keith's unit was constructed, such as central air conditioning, hardwood floors, and wood decks. Common areas include a newly opened pool and pool house, 4 tennis courts, and a nature trail through 15 acres of wooded land containing a stream-fed pond. It is considered a desireable condominium complex, competing with several nearby complexes having similar styles of units and common-area features.

The unit was recently reassessed by the town for $129,000, as were all the other B style units in the development.

Keith has included the following items in his application to the assessor:

1. A cover letter stating his opinion of value and summarizing the main reasons why he feels the condominium is too highly assessed.
2. The required property tax abatement form.
3. Photographs of the subject condominium and comparable condominiums.
4. A completed comparable sales approach to value for the subject condominium.
5. A completed cost approach to value for the subject condominium.
6. An equalization study summary.
7. A copy of the tax bill for the property.
8. A copy of certain sections of the Declaration of Condominium (the document which legally formed the condominium).

See Case 2, Exhibits A–N on pages 108–121.

                                          211 Winding Brook Lane
                                          Hamptonshire, NH

Town of Hamptonshire Assessor
Town Hall
123 Main Street
Hamptonshire, NH

Dear Sir:

    Enclosed is an Application for Abatement of Taxes on Unit
#211 at Summer Brook Condominiums, located at 211 Winding Brook
Lane, Map/lot No. 111-324. The property has been assessed at
$129,000, which I feel is greater than fair market value. For the
reasons outlined below, I believe a more reasonable assessed
value for this unit is $110,000.

1.   The unit is a "B" style unit. It appears that regarding
common area ownership it has been assessed as a larger and more
valuable "A-1" style unit.

2.   The property record card contains several descriptive
errors. It shows the unit as having central air conditioning, an
extra half bath and hardwood floors. These features are only
found in "B" style Units 307 through 309, which are of newer
construction.

3.   A cost approach shows a value for the unit of $113,370.

4.   Recent comparable sales of other similar condominiums
indicates a fair market value of about $115,500 for my unit.

5.   The most recent Rockingstone County Equalization Study shows
that the average condominiums assessment is still only 95% of
fair market value.

    I have attached a more detailed explanation of my findings
with this letter. I would appreciate your attention to
correcting what I feel to be an unfairly high assessment.

Best regards,

Keith McHugh

CASE 2. EXHIBIT A.

Additional Information

1. **"B" style unit**: I have attached to this application for abatement three pages reprinted from the recorded "Declaration of Condominium" which formed Summer Brook Condominiums. "Exhibit A" indicates that Unit 211 is a "B" style unit which has a 3.04% undivided interest in the common areas. "Schedule C" describes the layout of each style unit. The third page lists the common area ownership of all units. It shows that "A-1" style units have a 3.76% common area ownership interest.

The property record card shows that the total value of land at Summer Brook is $720,750, and the total value of common area amenities is $780,000. Applying a figure of 3.04% to these amounts shows that the proper assessment for Unit 211 for common area ownership of each is:

Land $720,750 × .0304 = $21,910

Amenities $780,000 × .0304 = $23,712

The property record card shows values of $27,100 (land) and $29,328 (amenities) which are the amounts that an "A-1" type unit should be assessed based on 3.76% common area ownership. Apparently the incorrect percentage was applied to my unit. The assessment for land and amenities is therefore $10,806 too high.

2. **Descriptive errors**: The condo unit assessment is several thousand dollars too high because it includes an extra bath, hardwood floors and central air conditioning, features not contained in Unit 211 (see "Schedule C", attached). My own cost approach using the same cost manual as the Town of Hamptonshire shows a value of $113,370 for the unit.

3. **Conclusion of market value**: I have placed more emphasis on the comparable sales approach, concluding a market value of $115,500. There were numerous recent condo sales, including two "B" unit sales at Summer Brook (identical to my unit) to support this amount.

4. **Equalization study**: Although the Town of Hamptonshire has indicated it intends to assess properties at 100% of fair market value, it has not yet done so. The latest Rockingstone County Equalization Study shows that the average condominium assessment is still about 95% of fair market value. Applying this figure to the fair market value of my unit results in what I feel is a fair and equitable assessed value of $110,000:

$115,500 × .95 = $110,000 (rounded).

CASE 2. EXHIBIT B.

Town of Hamptonshire

Application for Abatement of Taxes

Date filed __10-27-92__   Tax year __1992-93__

Name of
Applicant(s) __Keith McHugh__

_____

Property
Address __211 Winding Brook Lane__

Map - Lot Number __147-211-000__

Assessment __#129,000__

Reasons for filing abatment application:

> Property is assessed at more than market value.
> See attached letter and explanation.

Signature of applicant(s) __Keith McHugh__

_____

Mailing Address __211 Winding Brook Lane__

_____

Note: The filing of this application does not stay the collection of the taxes due. They should be paid as assessed by the due date. Refund will follow if abatement is allowed.

CASE 2. EXHIBIT C.

EXHIBIT "A"

Unit #211 of Summer Brook Condominiums, located on Winding Brook Lane, Hamptonshire, Rockingstone County, New Hampshire, as established by the within Grantor pursuant to New Hampshire RSA 356-B by Declaration of Condominium dated January 25, 1987 and recorded at the Rockingstone County Registry of Deeds at Volume 3107, Page 392.

Said Unit is laid out as shown on the Site Plan filed with the Declaration and is shown on the Floor Plan to be recorded simultaneously herewith. Unit #211 is a "B" style unit as described on the Floor Plan and further described in "Schedule C Unit Identification" as recorded simultaneously with the Floor Plan. Recorded together with such Floor Plan is the verified statement of a Licensed Professional Engineer in the manner required by New Hampshire RSA 356-B-20 (II).

Said Unit is hereby conveyed together with a 3.04% undivided interest in the Common Areas and Facilities appurtenant to said Unit as provided in the Declaration, together with the right to use the same in common with others entitled thereto, and is conveyed subject to the provisions of the Declaration and By-Laws and the rules and regulations adopted thereunder.

Said Unit is to be used only for residential purposes and shall not be used for any business purposes except as may be expressly permitted by the Board of Directors in accordance with the provisions of the Declaration and By-Laws.

Said Unit is acquired with the benefit of and subject to the provisions of New Hampshire RSA 356-B relating to Unit Ownership of real property as the statute is written as of the date hereof and as it may in the future be amended.

Being the same premises described in the deed of Richard B. Applegate to the mortgagors herein, dated March 11, 1986 and recorded in the Rockingstone County Registry of Deeds herewith.

CASE 2. EXHIBIT D.

(Added by the Twentieth Amendment)

SCHEDULE C

DESCRIPTION OF UNITS

All Summer Brook Condominium Residential Units contain two or three bedrooms. Depending upon the type of unit, each Residential Unit is comprised of approximately the following. There may be slight variations in layout and accessory areas from unit to unit. Only the recorded floor plans show exactly what each unit consists of, but to as great a degree as possible the following describe the various condominium Residential Units.

Two Bedroom Unit:

"A"

First Floor: Entry way, half bath, living room, dining room, kitchen, hallway, two bedrooms, full bath

Accessory: Garage, full basement

Living Area: 1,350 sq. ft.

Three Bedroom Unit:

"A-1"

First Floor: Entryway, hallway, half bath, washer/dryer room, breakfast room, kitchen, dining room, living room, master bedroom, master bath

Second Floor: Loft, bedroom, full bath

Accessory: two car garage, full basement, deck

Living Area: 2,275 sq. ft.

Two Bedroom Unit:

"B"

First Floor: Entryway, half bath, living room, dining room, kitchen, breakfast room, laundry room

Second Floor: Hallway, one full bath, two bedrooms, study

Accessory: Garage

Living Area: 1,840 sq. ft.

CASE 2.   EXHIBIT E.

Summer Brook Condominiums

Unit	Building	Type	Area of Unit (sq/ft)	% of Common Area Allocated to Unit
101	1	A	1,350	2.23
102	1	A	1,350	2.23
103	1	A	1,350	2.23
104	1	A-1	2,275	3.76
105	1	A-1	2,275	3.76
106	1	A-1	2,275	3.76
107	1	A-1	2,275	3.76
108	1	A-1	2,275	3.76
109	1	B	1,840	3.04
110	1	B	1,840	3.04
111	1	B	1,840	3.04
112	1	B	1,840	3.04
201	2	A	1,350	2.23
202	2	A	1,350	2.23
203	2	A	1,350	2.23
204	2	A	1,350	2.23
205	2	A	1,350	2.23
206	2	A-1	2,275	3.76
207	2	A-1	2,275	3.76
208	2	A-1	2,275	3.76
209	2	A-1	2,275	3.76
210	2	B	1,840	3.04
211	2	B	1,840	3.04
212	2	B	1,840	3.04
301	3	A	1,350	2.23
302	3	A	1,350	2.23
303	3	A	1,350	2.23
304	3	A-1	2,275	3.76
305	3	A-1	2,275	3.76
305	3	A-1	2,275	3.76
307	3	B	1,840	3.04
308	3	B	1,840	3.04
309	3	B	1,840	3.04

TOTALS:

33 UNITS			60,550 SQ. FT	100%

CASE 2.   EXHIBIT F.

211 Winding Brook Lane
Summer Brook Condominiums
Map - Lot # 147-211-000
Owner: Keith McHugh

Comparable "A"
Sable Lake Condominiums
(Typical Units)

CASE 2.   EXHIBIT G.

Comparable "B"
Stone Village Condominiums
(Typical Units)

Comparable "C"
Fisherman Cover Condominiums
(Typical Units)

CASE 2. EXHIBIT H.

FORM #4: COMPARABLE SALES

(NOTE: Unless otherwise noted, sales reflect all property rights, normal financing terms and arm's length transactions. For all other factors, make + or – dollar value adjustments in each row as appropriate.)

OWNER NAME(S): Keith McHugh   (Page 1 of 2)

SUBJECT PROPERTY ADDRESS: 211 Winding Brook Lane

SUBJECT MAP AND PARCEL NUMBER: 147 – 211 – 000

	COMPARABLE same as subject		COMPARABLE same as subject		COMPARABLE A	
1. Property Address	110 Winding La.		212 Winding La.		13 Sable Lake	
2. Sale Price	115,500		114,900		120,000	
3. Date of Sale / + or –	2 mos.		2 mos.		3 mos.	
4. Location / + or –	similar		similar		similar	
5. Home SQ/FT Size / + or –	same		same		same	
6. Number of Rooms / + or –	same		same		same	
7. Number of Baths / + or –	1		1		1½	– 2,500
8. Garage / + or –	Yes/car		Yes/car		Yes/car	
9. Pool / + or –						
10. Deck or Porch / + or –	No		No		Yes	– 1,500
11. Basement / + or –	Full		Full		Full	
12. Fireplace / + or –	Yes		Yes		Yes	
13. Other Features / + or –						
14. Age / + or –	5 yrs		5 yrs		5 yrs	
15. Condition / + or –	EX		EX		EX	
16. Land / + or –						
FINAL ADJUSTED SALES PRICE	115,500		114,900		116,000	

CASE 2. EXHIBIT I.

FORM #4: COMPARABLE SALES

(NOTE: Unless otherwise noted, sales reflect all property rights, normal financing terms and arm's length transactions. For all other factors, make + or − dollar value adjustments in each row as appropriate.)

OWNER NAME(S): _Keith McHugh_

(Page 2 of 2)

SUBJECT PROPERTY ADDRESS: _211 Winding Brook Lane_

SUBJECT MAP AND PARCEL NUMBER: _147−211−000_

	COMPARABLE _B_		COMPARABLE _B_		COMPARABLE _C_	
1. Property Address	24 Stone Village		102 Stone Village		14 Fisherman Cove	
2. Sale Price	114,000		116,500		115,000	
3. Date of Sale / + or −	2 mos		3 mos		2 mos	
4. Location / + or −	similar		similar		similar	
5. Home SQ/FT Size / + or −	similar		similar		similar	
6. Number of Rooms / + or −	same		same		same	
7. Number of Baths / + or −	1		1½	−2,500	1	
8. Garage / + or −	Yes		Yes		Yes	
9. Pool / + or −						
10. Deck or Porch / + or −	No		No		Yes	−1,500
11. Basement / + or −	Full		Full		Full	
12. Fireplace / + or −	No	+1400	Yes		Yes	
13. Other Features / + or −						
14. Age / + or −	6 yrs		6 yrs		4 yrs	
15. Condition / + or −	Ex		Ex		Ex	
16. Land / + or −						
FINAL ADJUSTED SALES PRICE	115,400		114,000		113,500	

CASE 2. EXHIBIT J.

1992 REAL PROPERTY TAX BILL
TOWN OF HAMPTONSHIRE, NH

Office of the Collector of Taxes
123 Main Street
Town Hall
Hamptonshire, NH

OFFICE HOURS:
9:OO TO 5:00
MON. to FRI.

Tax payable at collector's office
or by mail. Include SELF ADDRESSED
STAMPED ENVELOPE for receipt if
desired.

TAX DUE DATE: NOVEMBER 20

TAX RATE PER $1000	RESID.	COMM.	INDUST.	VACANT	PROPERTY IDENTIFICATION	TAXPAYER IDENTIFICATION	EXEMPTIONS	CLASS
Town	$7.47	$9.75	$9.75	$1.48	PARCEL #: 147-211-000	Keith McHugh	02 Veteran	Resid.
County	$0.95	$2.85	$2.85	$0.95	TAX BILL #: 3507	211 Winding Brook Lane		
Schools	$6.12	$6.46	$6.46	$4.25	LOCATION:	Hamptonshire, NH		
Sewer	$2.21	$2.21	$2.21	$2.21	211 Winding Brook Lane			
TOTAL	$16.75	$21.27	$21.27	$8.89				

LAND VALUE	BUILDING VALUE	TOTAL VALUE	TOTAL TAX	TOTAL EXEMPTIONS	TOTAL PAYMENT DUE
$27,100	$101,914	$129,014	$2,161.98	$250.00	$1,910.98

TAXES ARE DUE IN FULL ON DUE DATE. UNPAID TAXES ARE SUBJECT TO 12% INTEREST AFTER DUE DATE

CASE 2. EXHIBIT K.

FORM #5: COST APPROACH WORKSHEET

Owner Name(s): ___Keith McHugh___

Property Address: ___211 Winding Brook Lane___

Property Map & Parcel Number: ___147-211-000___

VALUE OF IMPROVEMENTS

AREA 1: Residence

1. ___1,230___ sq/ft × $ ___48.78___ per sq/ft = $ ___60,000___
   (Living area)   (Cost per sq/ft)   (Cost of living area)

   ___610___
   (basement)   ×   ___10.66___   = $ ___6,503___

AREA 2: Non-living area (garage, screened porch etc.)

2. ___180___ sq/ft × $ ___18.95___ per sq/ft = $ ___3,411___
   (Non-living area)   (Cost per sq/ft)   (Cost of non-living area)

3. TOTAL of lines 2 and 3: $ ___69,914___

4.   Amounts for extra features:

      Fireplace $ ___1,400___

      Pool $ _____

      Patio $ _____

      Other Special Features $ _____

5. TOTAL of lines 3 and 4: $ ___71,314___
   (Replacement Cost New)

6. Minus depreciation amount: − $ ___5% (− 3,566)___

7. Current Value of Improvement $ ___67,748___

VALUE OF LAND

8. Value of Land ___(+ condo ammenities)___ $ ___45,622___

9. TOTAL value of property
   (line 7 + line 8): $ ___113,370___

CASE 2.   EXHIBIT L.

Parcel #: 147-211-000	RECORD OF OWNERSHIP	DATE	BOOK	PAGE	PRICE	Class	RES
211 Winding Brook Lane	Richard B. Applegate	3-11-86	3107	392	84,600	Zoning	R1
OWNER: Keith McHugh	Keith McHugh	4-6-91	3511	314	108,000	Use	SFR
211 Winding Brook Lane						NH Code	RES
Hamptonshire, NH							

INSPECTION WITNESSED BY:

ASSESSMENT RECORD

	1988	1992	19	19	19	19	19	19	Visit History
Building	38,000	69,345							Don Blake – 6-7-88
Garage/Non-living	4,000	3,241							
Other (Condo amenities)	4,000	29,328							
TOTAL VALUE BUILDING	46,000	101,914							
TOTAL VALUE LAND	14,600	27,100							
TOTAL LAND & BUILDING	60,000	129,014							

LAND VALUE COMPUTATIONS AND SUMMARY

Description	Code	Size	Rate	Influence Factor	Land Value
Primary site	C/L	1 unit	27,100	—	27,100
Secondary site					
Undeveloped					
Marshland					
Waterfront					
TOTALS					

Property Factors

TOPOGRAPHY		STREET	
Level	✓	Paved	✓
Hilly		Sidewalk	✓
Swampy		Unpaved	
NEIGHBORHOOD		IMPROVEMENTS	
Improving	✓	Water	✓
Static		Electric	✓
Declining		Sewer	✓

NOTES: See master card for description of land and amenities.

Total value of land and amenities = $780,000   6-15-91   D. Blake

Total land value = $720,750   6-15-91

CASE 2. EXHIBIT M.

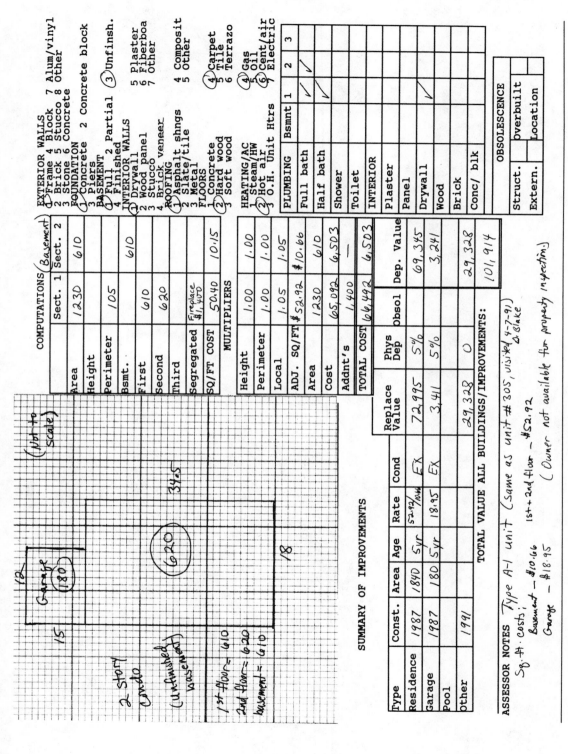

EXTERIOR WALLS
1 Frame 4 Block 7 Alum/vinyl
2 Brick 5 Stucco 8 Other
3 Stone 6 Concrete
FOUNDATION
1 Concrete 2 Concrete block
3 Piers
BASEMENT
1 Full 2 Partial ③ Unfinsh.
4 Finished
INTERIOR WALLS
1 Drywall 5 Plaster
2 Wood panel 6 Fiberboa
3 Stucco 7 Other
4 Brick veneer
ROOFING
1 Asphalt,shngs 4 Composit
2 Slate/tile 5 Other
3 Metal
FLOORS
1 Concrete ④ Carpet
2 Hard wood 5 Tile
3 Soft wood 6 Terrazo
HEATING/AC
1 Steam/HW ④ Gas
2 Hot air 5 Oil
③ O.H. Unit Htrs ⑥ Cent/air
7 Electric

COMPUTATIONS (Basement)

	Sect. 1	Sect. 2
Area	1230	610
Height		
Perimeter	105	
Bsmt.	610	
First	610	
Second	620	
Third		
Segregated	Fireplace $1,400	
SQ/FT COST	50.40	10.15

MULTIPLIERS

Height	1.00	1.00
Perimeter	1.00	1.00
Local	1.05	1.05
ADJ. SQ/FT	$52.92	$10.66
Area	1230	610
Cost	65,092	6,503
Addnt's	1,400	—
TOTAL COST	66,492	6,503

PLUMBING	1	2	3
Bsmnt		✓	
Full bath	✓		
Half bath		✓	
Shower			
Toilet			
INTERIOR			
Plaster			
Panel			
Drywall		✓	
Wood			
Brick			
Conc/ blk			

OBSOLESCENCE	
Struct.	overbuilt
Extern.	Location

SUMMARY OF IMPROVEMENTS

Type	Const.	Area	Age	Rate	Cond	Replace Value	Phys Dep	Obsol	Dep. Value
Residence	1987	1840	5yr	52.92/sqm	EX	72,995	5%		69,345
Garage	1987	180	5yr	18.95	EX	3.41	5%		3,241
Pool									
Other	1991					29,328	0		29,328

TOTAL VALUE ALL BUILDINGS/IMPROVEMENTS: 101,914

ASSESSOR NOTES Type A-1 unit (same as unit #305, visited 4-7-91) D.Blake
Sq. ft. costs: 1st + 2nd floor — $52.92
Basement — $10.66
Garage — $18.95
(Owner not available for property inspection.)

CASE 2. EXHIBIT N.

Go Ask the Assessor

Ask and learn.
THE APOCRYPHA

We asked some assessors, chosen randomly from assessing jurisdictions throughout the country, for their opinions on the property taxation process.

We were interested in getting a feeling for how assessors think about certain subjects. We weren't out to prove or disprove anything. Only to gather some opinions and perhaps some feedback from assessors that you, the homeowner, might find helpful.

In the following pages, some of these assessors share their experience and knowledge about how residential taxpayers can ensure the accuracy of their tax assessment and present the best case for a tax reduction.

Although some of the comments are specific to particular states, what is most interesting is that much of their advice can be applied almost anywhere.

Roland G. Register
Eight years experience
Tax Administrator
State Certified Assessor
New Hanover County, North Carolina

The biggest problem with the property owner is lack of knowledge and understanding about the process.

I find the typical resident doesn't understand the "mass appraisal" concept, nor do they understand the use of funds. The response ranges from fair to poor. As for their representation by consultants, this has no bearing on the final decision, whether represented or not. Consultants who work on a contingency and lead homeowners to believe everyone can get a tax reduction provide "disservice" instead of service. Their approach is usually to ask for a reduction, regardless of the relationship of the appraisal to market value. The homeowner is let down and frustrated with the government because he was led to believe the consultant could get the value lowered. On the other hand, keen professionals can survey similar properties, understand the mass appraisal methods, and assist the appraiser and the homeowner in determining if an inequity exists. That is "service."

Intimidation by appealing rather than working informally with the assessor does not increase results for the owner; it only makes the process formal. Consultants who do not work with assessors to resolve differences informally end up with delays in having a formal board rule on the client's property. We do not ask the Board to digest last-minute statistics and detail and provide instant response. If there is any conflict with appraisal, we suggest a delay or reschedule for the hearing.

What are my feelings about taxpayer knowledge? They do not understand mass appraisal, market value, and enough about government to understand who provides what services out of which source of revenue. They can't separate the concept of "value" from the relationship with "taxes." With revaluation to market value having several years in the cycle, owners get lulled into thinking the "tax value" is always less than the "market value." Then, they cannot understand why "mass" appraisal is not as precise as "fee" appraisal. Since local government is the closest "ear," locals get the blame for all the governmental fallacies, regardless of whose responsibility relates to the taxpayer's complaint.

In summary, the biggest problem with the property owner is lack of knowledge and understanding about the process. The biggest problem with nonprofessional tax consultants is that most substitute aggressiveness for knowledge and professionalism.

We now have 67,000 parcels revalued for 1991. There were 27 formal appeals to the Board of Equalization and Review, mostly commercial property owners. Only four appeals have been made to the state level.

Professionals are welcomed in my office, and I believe our reputation in the community has been enhanced by their opinions.

Betty M. Peck
18 Years Experience
Assessor
Coconino County Assessor's Office
Flagstaff Arizona

Taxpayers should verify public records before they file an appeal.

In the State of Arizona, the full cash value (assessed value) and the market value of a property are synonymous. Check to see if the full cash value of the property is greater than the market value. If it is, then you should file an appeal to have the property reviewed. If the full cash value of the property is lower than the market value, quite probably there is no need to file an appeal.

In Arizona, the full cash value and the assessment ratio are the areas to check carefully to be sure they are correct. Taxpayers should verify public records before they file an appeal. They should check:

1. Age of the structure
2. Number of ft^2 in the structure
3. Number of bedrooms in the structure
4. Number of rooms in the structure
5. Type of materials used in construction
6. Quality of workmanship in construction
7. Size of land area
8. Location of property
9. Most current sale price.

We often see the statement the taxes are too high in an appeal. This is really not an item that can be reviewed, since the tax rates change annually and are not set until several months after the appeal period.

When preparing an appeal, the taxpayer should show at least three comparable properties, using the nine points listed above, that may have a lower value than the subject property. State in the appeal which, if any, areas of the public record are incorrect and be willing to allow an ad valorem appraiser to inspect the property to verify your statements and to correct the public record.

In Arizona, the property value increases are limited to a maximum of 10 percent annually until the limited value and the full cash value become equal. This is a formula listed in statue, and is not an area that can be appealed unless there is a mathematical error.

Kayle J. Depoy
22 Years Experience
Certified Assessor Level IV
C.R.A. Senior Appraiser of N.A.R.A
City of Muskegon Assessing Office
Muskegon, Michigan

If the public votes a five mill increase on school operation, they have voted themselves a tax increase.

The property owner should first check the data on the assessor's appraisal card for accuracy. Verify the dimensions, see if the listing of attributes is correct, such as bathrooms, fireplaces, etc. Also find out the classification rating such as average, substandard, or superior construction and design, and how much depreciation is presently being granted.

The second item the property owner must have is documented proof of current market values within his homogenous neighborhood area. These should not be isolated incidence of sale but the usual selling price within his general area. These sales should also represent "arm's length" transactions, not private sales, estate sales, or sales of duress. This requires a certain amount of time researching selling activity in the area.

Then make a reasonable comparison of the sale properties to the homeowner's property. This would include the size of the lot as well as size of the dwelling. Very important, also, is the age of the comparison. Allow for differences in the quality and design of the homes, as well as the amenities such as fireplaces, number of bathrooms, bedrooms, garage space, finished basement area, etc.

Item number three. Citizens should understand that taxes are a combination of assessments and millages which are allowed either by state property-tax laws, charters, or by a ballot that the property owners participate in. If the public votes a five mill increase on school operation, they have voted themselves a tax increase.

Item four. Many homeowners are unaware of state rebates on homesteads and the federal tax deduction available. The following example is relative in the State of Michigan:

If a property with a market value of $80,000 is assessed at $40,000, the local tax rate is 70 mills per $1000, the owners of the property have a "household income" of $50,000, and the property owner is not a senior citizen, the rebate is as follows: deduct three and one-half percent of household income from the homestead tax, then take 60 percent of the difference for the rebate. Thus, 70 mills times the $40,000 assessment make a tax of $2800. Three and one-half percent of $50,000 (income) is $1750. This subtracted from the tax is $1050. Sixty percent of the remainder leaves $630 for the refund.

Now, regarding the Federal tax benefit, the $50,000 income would be subject to the 28 percent tax bracket. There would be a tax savings of $784 in Federal income tax. With the $630 refund and the $784 in Federal tax savings, the net amount in taxes is $1385, less than one-half of the original amount. Now, had the owners in the above illustration been senior citizens, the amount of the state rebate would have been the entire difference of $1050. Therefore, the senior would have had a net tax of $966.

Kit Carson Weaver
15 Years Experience
Carson City Assessor
Accredited Nevada Appraiser
Carson City, Nevada

Be calm and stick to the facts only.

Taxpayers need to know the laws and use the tax laws to protect against an overassessment. They should:

1. Visit local assessor or state taxation office to get *written* laws on property assessment, even if there is a cost involved.

2. Have copies made of all statistical information used to appraise their property. (Lot size, house and garage square footage, yard improvements, heat source, pool cover, etc.)

3. Take information home, review assessment laws, call state or assessor to clarify when necessary. *Remeasure* and *recalculate* all assessor information, inform assessor of any discrepancies, file appeal if correction not made.

4. Research sales prices on comparable properties. (Check with county recorder, realtors, etc.) Most states do not allow appraised values to exceed market (full cash) value.

5. Take a knowledgeable person with you to the Board of Equalization hearing. *Be calm and stick to the facts only.*

Max R. Lenington
21 Years Experience
Yellowstone County Assessor
Certified Montana Assessor
Billings, Montana

View the assessor's office as an ally, not an adversary.

Taxpayers are justifiably concerned about rising property taxes. But how can anger at higher taxes be turned into effective protest and a successful appeal of assessed value? Act according to three important principles and you may halt rising taxes and file a successful appeal. Even if you can't change anything, you will understand more about what really needs to be changed.

1. Separate the issue of higher taxes from the issue of the accuracy of the assessed value of your property. Elected officials, school boards, and other special taxing authorities establish your tax bill. Assessors estimate the market value of you property. An increase in value doesn't mean your taxes will go up.

2. Understand how the assessor arrived at the value of your property. If you do file an appeal, this information will help you construct your case. Find several properties similar to yours (called comparables), preferably in the same neighborhood. Find out what their assessed values are or the prices at which they sold, if they have sold recently.

3. Establish a cooperative, not an adversarial, relationship with the assessor's office. The office can and will provide you with the information you need to evaluate your assessment, find similar properties, and file your appeal. Be sure to follow instructions carefully. A missed deadline or incorrect filing can cause an appeal to be dismissed.

The assessor unfairly bears the brunt of anger about rising taxes. But yelling at the assessor about your tax bill is as effective as yelling at your mail carrier because the price of postage stamps has gone up. The assessor's job is narrower than most taxpayers believe. Assessors don't decide how much tax is to be paid and they don't establish tax rates. Their task is to estimate, as accurately as possible, the market value of your property.

Pretend for a moment that the assessor's estimation of the value of your property is the highest price you would be allowed to accept if you sold. If that were so, you would be much more concerned about the accuracy of the valuation than the affect on your tax bill. If you can keep pretending, you will have the right framework for your discussion with the assessor. You will be both clearly focused on determining if the value of your property has been accurately estimated. You will be able to see the problem more clearly and understand if and how the assessor's office is at fault.

You may still be angry about the size of your tax bill. To mount an effective protest against high property taxes, you need to concentrate your efforts on your city council, school board—or whoever creates budgets and sets tax rates. These officials determine how much money the property tax has to raise each year.

The tax rate is a relationship between the amount of taxes to be raised and the tax base. The tax rate is calculated by dividing the tax base (the total assessed value of all taxable property in jurisdiction) into the amount of tax that must be raised. For example, if total assessed value is $100 million and the amount of tax to be raised is $1 million, the tax rate is 1 percent. If total assessed value doubles, and the amount of tax to be raised stays at $1 million, the tax rate drops to 0.5 percent. In this case, if your property has increased in value, your tax remains the same. However, if assessed value doubles to $200 million and the tax rate stays at 1 percent, the amount to be collected in taxes doubles to $2 million. In this case, if your property has increased in value, you will probably pay more tax.

If officials claim they are not raising taxes because the tax rate remains the same, the taxpayer should be wary. The question to ask officials is how much total assessed value has changed. If total assessed value has risen, then a tax increase has been "enacted" even though the tax rate remains the same.

The next question to ask is whether increased services or the increased costs of services justify increased taxes. You may decide that you are willing to pay more taxes for an improved school system or better police or fire protection. These are complex questions that must be addressed to the appropriate officials—not to the assessor.

Assessors estimate the fair market value of a property, that is, the price most people would pay for it in its condition as of the assessment date. The best indicator of fair market value is market activity. Buyers and sellers create market value by their transactions. In an appeal, the best evidence of market value is sale price—the sale price of the subject property or of similar properties (called comparables).

However, sale price is not necessarily the same as market value. The assessor carefully examines all sales, and adjusts them for special circumstances that might decrease or inflate prices. An owner in a hurry to sell might sell for less. If the seller includes substantial personal property in the sale or provides discounted financing, the sale price is likely to be inflated. Although the sales comparison approach is not the only approach used (cost and income approaches are two others), comparable sales are recognized by courts as the best evidence of market value. Residential taxpayers who appeal successfully, usually do by finding comparable properties that have lower assessed values, or that have recently sold for less than the assessed values.

Many taxpayers are angered at increases in assessed values because the property has not changed. But physical change is not the only reason for a change in property value. The market is. If a town's major industry leaves, property values collapse. Conversely, as decaying neighborhoods with good housing stock are discovered by young homeowners, prices gradually rise, and then soar as the neighborhood becomes fashionable. A shortage of detached houses in a desireable city neighborhood can send prices to ridiculous levels. In a recession, larger homes may stay on the market for a long time, but two-bedroom condominiums are in demand, so their prices rise. In a stable neighborhood, with no extraordinary pressure from the market, inflation increases property values. Home buyers, home sellers, bank appraisers, real estate analysts, and the assessor all pay attention to the same market factors in valuing property.

The first step in valuation is data collection. The assessor's office collects quantities of information about each property in the jurisdiction. The information is recorded on a property record form, which may be reviewed for accuracy by the taxpayer.

The assessor's office also collects sales data and data on social, economic, and environmental factors affecting property value, for example, employment, population and income patterns, interest rates, construction costs, regional location factors (such as access to parks, churches, schools, and public transportation), zoning, and rent control. Complete and accurate maps are essential to the assessor's office. Many jurisdictions now have computerized geographic information systems that are used by many branches of government. These systems integrate ownership records with information about zoning, sewage systems, land use, soil types, communication networks, geologic structure, and a host of other data.

In short, the assessor's office has an abundance of data relevant to the value of your property. Incidentally, this information makes the office an important community resource.

To apply this information to valuing property, the assessor constructs a model—a simplified representation of how market factors affect value. Most residential property is valued with a cost model or a sales comparison model.

A cost model says the estimated value of your property equals the value of the land and cost of constructing a replacement, less depreciation. Replacement cost is usually found by a cost manual that shows regional construction costs for all building elements. Depreciation depends largely on age, condition, and the current desirability of the property's features and location. Sales comparison models are usually more important in appeals. A sales comparison model says the estimated market value of your property equals the sale price of a comparable property, with adjustments to the sale price for differences between your property and the comparable. For example, if your property has a swimming pool and two bathrooms, but the comparable has no pool and three bathrooms, you would add the value of the pool to the comparable's sale price and subtract the value of the bathroom. The result would be evidence of what you might expect to sell your property for.

Assessors use more than one comparable, usually three to five. Also, they use more complex models that incorporate many more factors. And rather than considering properties one at a time, assessors use computer software to appraise at one time many properties of the same general type, for example, townhouses or raised ranches.

Every jurisdiction has an appeals process mandated by law. The first step is usually an informal meeting with someone in the assessor's office. (Sometimes this informal review is handled by telephone or mail.) Information on the mechanics and deadlines for setting up an appointment should be included with your assessment notice, along with similar information for the entire appeals process. During or before this informal meeting, you should review the property record form on your property to be sure all the information is correct. Know the lot size, number of stories, square footage, and condition of your property. If you have an accurate survey of your property, be sure to bring it with you to the meeting. You may also want to identify comparable properties and review their record forms.

The person conducting the meeting will probably give you information on comparable properties. If you have assembled information on such properties, you should bring it to the meeting. Almost all the information in the assessor's office is available to the public, and the office can help you find comparable properties.

Your aims at this informal review—which is not yet an appeal—should be (1) to verify the information on your property record form, or correct it, (2) to make sure you understand how your value was arrived at, (3) to discover if the value is fair compared with the values of similar properties in your neighborhood, (4) to find out if you qualify for any exemptions, and (5) to be sure you understand how to file a formal appeal and how the office can help you, if you still want to appeal.

The assessor would always prefer to settle problems at the informal review. Appeals are costly, and assessors usually have tight budgets. The person conducting the meeting may not commit to a change in value at this meeting, even though you have uncovered an error or all agree that the assessment is not fair. The decision about a value change may have to be made by someone else and communicated to you in writing. If this is so, find out when you may expect to hear from the office.

The first level of formal appeal is usually to a local board. Your appeal is more likely to be successful if you present evidence that comparable properties in the same neighborhood are assessed for less than yours. Copies of property record forms on your comparables, with records of their assessed values or sales prices are your best defense. Note any differences between your property and the comparables and point out these differences. The appeal board will be interested only in the fairness and the accuracy of the value placed on your property, not in whether you can afford to pay your taxes or whether taxes are too high.

If you disagree with the local board's decision, the next, and the highest, level of administrative review is a state tax tribunal. After that, unresolved legal issues may be taken to the state supreme court. Residential appeals are usually settled at the local level.

Always remember to view the assessor's office as an ally, not an adversary. Employees of the office should have been trained to be calm, polite, and helpful, but they are only human. If you can be calm and polite, they are likely to be more helpful and can concentrate on giving you the information you need for a successful appeal.

Meeting with the Assessor or Appeal Board

A compromise is the art of dividing a cake in such a way that everyone believes that he has got the biggest piece.
DR. LUDWIG ERHARD (1897–1977),
East German politician

This chapter contains two parts. The first is a general discussion about meetings with assessors, and appearances before appeal boards. It contains some useful tips on what to expect at these meetings, and how to best prepare for them. The second part is a collection of appeal board case summaries. These brief snapshots of actual appeal board cases show what the main issues were in each case, and why the boards decided as they did. The examples were selected to demonstrate a range of issues which boards typically decide.

Informal Meeting with the Assessor

Most jurisdictions allow for some period of time in which a taxpayer may meet informally with the assessor to work out differences of opinion. Appendix A, "Individual State Information" contains a list of the appeal levels available in each state. Since laws and procedures are subject to change every year, however, check with your local assessor to see what appeal options are currently available to you.

Preparing to meet with the assessor need not be particularly difficult. You will, however, need a certain amount of perseverance and the ability to focus on the main points of your arguments. For this, and all levels of appeal, your best offense will be strong arguments, backed by solid evidence, supporting your opinion of value.

Emotion should play no part in your dealings with the assessor or other public officials. While the injustice of your assessment may seem worthy of an impassioned appearance before the Supreme Court, to the assessor it is just another technical problem to be resolved. He or she usually has an interest in seeing that it is resolved in a reasonable manner. Keeping your emotions in check and staying focused on the real issues will go a long way towards assuring that you are given a fair hearing.

Even though the first stage of the appeal process in your area may be an informal meeting with the assessor, there is one formality that should still be observed. That is the filing, in a timely manner, of any appeal forms required in your tax district. Failure to do so may prevent you from proceeding to higher levels of appeal if you are not satisfied with the results of the first level.

In nearly all states, the burden of proof is on the taxpayer seeking to appeal an assessment. This means that the assessment on your property is presumed to be correct until you show, through overwhelming evidence, that it is not. Therefore, if both you and the assessor have equally valid arguments, the "house" (assessor) wins. Again, preparation is the key to success. (California makes an exception to the burden of proof rule for owner occupied, single family dwellings. There, the burden is on the assessor to prove that the property is correctly valued, in an appeal proceeding.)

Be prepared to accept some kind of compromise solution after meeting with the assessor. Unless your case is predicated on an obvious mechanical error that the assessor admits to completely, you will likely be offered a middle-ground solution at this point. Assessors have an uncanny knack for knowing how much of an adjustment to offer. It may be just enough to satisfy you and keep you from appealing at the next level. In fact, the vast majority of property tax disputes are settled at this stage, many through compromise. A relatively small percentage of cases proceed to higher appeal levels.

Whether or not to accept a compromise is a personal decision. If you feel you have an airtight case that can't possibly fail to sway an appeal board, go ahead and appeal. If your case is good, but not completely bullet proof, a compromise prior to the next appeal level may be the best solution you can hope to reach.

Assessors are sometimes willing to compromise even though your case may not be especially strong. There are several reasons for this. Preparing a rebuttal to your appeal is time-consuming, extra work for the already busy assessor. He or she may fear looking bad if too many total assessments wind up before a board of review, especially erroneous assessments. Lastly, there is always some chance of loosing any particular appeal before a board sympathetic to taxpayers. An assessor's compromise offer will be a modest one if your supporting evidence is not very compelling.

If you do come to a compromise agreement with the assessor, get it in writing before the deadline to bring your case to the next appeal level has expired. An informal oral agreement to adjust your assessment could be forgotten or interpreted differently at a later date if not recorded.

Appeal Boards

The majority of states now have property tax appeal levels that include a board of review style forum. While these boards follow certain guidelines and procedures in hearing appeals, they generally operate under far less formal rules of procedure than do the courts. This allows greater access to justice to a wider range of individuals. Many individuals would not pursue property-tax appeals if required to hire a lawyer at greater cost than the possible award. Unfortunately, certain states have not yet seen the wisdom of this arrangement, making it difficult for some property owners to cost-effectively appeal unfair property assessments. In other states, property owners have a choice between appealing to a property-tax board of review, or a state court, but not both.

Boards usually do not require the aggrieved taxpayer to appear in person. If you desire, you can submit your entire case to the board through the mail (certified mail with a reply is best.) You may also choose to be represented by someone else, although certain states limit who may represent you. For example, some allow property-tax consultants or family members to appear in your stead, while others do not. Usually a "letter of agency," or similar form, authorizing another to represent you will be required. Lawyers are allowed to represent taxpayers in all states.

If you choose self-representation, attend some board hearings before your own. This will allow you to get the "lay of the land" under less anxious conditions. You will get a feel for the kinds of questions board members are likely to ask, and you may pick up other important information as well.

Besides sitting in on board hearings, you may also be able to review a board's previous written decisions. These are normally available in either state or county offices and are open to public inspection. An hour or two spent browsing through these records will give you a good idea of the kinds of arguments that have won and lost appeals similar to your own.

If you appear before an appeal board, you can expect about a ten to fifteen minute chance to plead your case. Boards usually have very full schedules and want to hear the facts of the appeal stated as succinctly as possible. Be sure to have enough copies of your application and supporting material so that each board member has an individual copy. You can anticipate being asked whatever questions board members feel are appropriate.

You may or may not have the chance to ask questions of the assessor or the assessor's witnesses. Boards in some states will allow either side to subpoena witnesses whose testimony may be critical to the case.

Your oral statements should stick to the main points of your appeal. Avoid the temptation to lecture to board members about pet peeves that have no bearing on the facts of your case, such as local politics, high tax rates, or the assessor's lifestyle. Doing so will do nothing to win board member's support for the really important points you should be making. And, just as with your earlier meetings with the assessor, keep your emotions well in check.

Some appeal boards currently are operating as much as several years behind in hearing appeals. It is possible that your case may not be scheduled for a hearing until several years from the date you have filed the appeal. If this is so in your area, you will be required to pay all taxes on your property when due. If you eventually win your appeal you will be issued a tax refund with interest for the period of time you waited.

If your appeal is pending over more than one tax year, consider submitting a new appeal application to the board for each new tax year. Although winning certain kinds of appeals results in the lower assessment carrying forth into later years, usually the results of a tax appeal are applied only to the particular tax year in question. It is possible to win in one year and have the property assessment revert to its original value in the following year.

Some boards will combine in one hearing all of the appeals a taxpayer may have filed over several years for one property. If essentially the same facts and evidence are being used to support each year's claim, the board may combine them in the interest of expediency.

An appeal board will sometimes make, and announce its decision immediately upon the conclusion of the hearing. More often, however, you will have to wait for its written decision, which can take some time.

An important point to remember is that, often, appeal boards only consider the arguments and evidence presented at the prior level, or levels of appeal. If you filed an application for a property-tax abatement with the town or county which was denied, the board may simply review the reasons for the denial. Its review will be based on the evidence you originally submitted and new evidence may not be allowed. If you later come across other, more compelling evidence favoring your position, you may not be able to present it to the board.

Some boards will consider previously unsubmitted evidence from both the taxpayer and the assessor. In this regard it is a good idea to learn how the various appeal levels work in your area before committing yourself. The best advice to follow, however, is simple: present convincing arguments and evidence at the first level, since this may be all you have to rely on at later appeal stages.

Homeowner and Condominium Associations

If you belong to a homeowner or condominium association, consider appealing your property-tax assessments as a group. If you don't currently belong to such an organization, consider forming one in your area for the specific purpose of appealing inequitable tax assessments.

Some reasons for doing so include:

- A stronger, more effective voice. It is true that the squeaky wheel gets the oil, and assessors will take notice of well-organized group appeals.

- The required research can be split up between a number of individuals, making the overall process easier.

- Members of the group having particular expertise, such as real estate agents, accountants, or lawyers can offer professional insight that, otherwise, might not be readily available.

- If it is necessary to hire professional help such as appraisers, lawyers, or tax consultants, the cost can be split between all members of the group. It may be possible to negotiate less expensive group terms with these professionals.

In the case of condominiums, the most effective case for assessment reductions will normally be made as a group. It is sometimes difficult, although not impossible, for an individual owner to prove that his or her assessment is unfair when other units in the project are similarly assessed. However, a condominium association, arguing that the entire development is assessed more highly than other condominium developments, stands a better chance of succeeding.

Selected Case Summaries

There are two points worth mentioning that are not readily apparent from reading the following summaries. One, it has been estimated that the majority of appeals that are filed with many county or state boards of review are settled prior to being heard by the boards. If you review the files of your own local or state appeal board, you will probably find them filled with letters withdrawing appeal applications. This is often the result of compromise agreements between taxpayers and the local assessor, sometimes prompted by the filing of the appeal to the board.

Secondly, the most common reason for denial of an appeal will be the taxpayer's failure to submit the appeal by the deadline date, or in the required form. Boards usually have a backlog of cases to hear and will simply rule against one which does not fulfill the proper procedural filing requirements.

Case 1: New Hampshire Board of Tax & Land Appeals (BTLA) Docket #6358-89

Fact summary. The taxpayers appealed the town's assessed value of $60,650 (land, $1900; buildings $58,750). The appeal was based on the price paid by the taxpayers three years earlier of $149,000. They argued that the state's equalization study indicated the town had assessed the market value of the property at $466,538 and ". . this is far in excess of even recently built homes costing more."

Appeal board decision. In favor of the taxpayers. The board stated that "The taxpayers have the burden of showing that the assessment was disproportionately high or unlawful, resulting in the taxpayers paying an unfair and disproportionate share of taxes." The board discovered that the town had made a gross error in determining the size of the land being assessed.

Main issues involved. (1) Whether the taxpayers had satisfied the burden of proof requirement, and; (2) whether the property's assessed value was properly calculated for the tax year in question by working back from a later year's assessment calculations.

Comments. The decision demonstrates the taxpayers' satisfaction of the burden of proof requirement. In doing so, the taxpayers showed the value of an equalization study as support for a finding of overassessment.

The taxpayers were clearly correct in appealing this. The town made a gross land measurement error (mechanical error) in excess of *18 acres*. The taxpayers were also able to show that the assessed value of the property, even accounting for the measurement error, was much higher than other properties in its class, based on an equalization study.

Case 2: New Hampshire BTLA Docket #4460-88

Fact summary. This was a request by the taxpayers for a rehearing of an appeal previously submitted to the board. The grounds for the request was the taxpayers' assertion that they were denied due process of the law because they were not allowed to cross-examine a witness for the town. Prior to the original hearing the taxpayers were informed by the board that the witness would not be required to appear in person. They were advised, however, that they had the right to subpoena him.

Appeal board decision. Against the taxpayers. Noting that the taxpayers made "numerous unsubstantiated allegations of wrongdoing by public officials" and their assertion that "... the Board took the easy way out and denied us fair and equitable treatment," the written decision takes pains to express the Board's displeasure with the way the taxpayers conducted themselves at the original hearing. They used more than 5 hours in presenting their case, which the Board notes is "far in excess of the average time consumed per case before this Board."

Main issues involved. Whether the taxpayers were denied due process by not being able to question the witness.

Comments. The taxpayers claimed a legal error as the grounds for the appeal. The appeal failed, however, because the taxpayers did not subpoena the witness to appear at the original hearing, which was their right. Since they did not do so originally, they could not claim that due process had been violated at the hearing, and, therefore, no legal error had occurred.

In other respects, this is a good example of how not to conduct an appearance before a board. The taxpayers antagonized the members by making "unsubstantiated allegations" and by bombarding them with what was apparently a large quantity of irrelevant information that did not support their allegations.

Case 3: New Hampshire BTLA Docket #6224-89

Fact summary. The taxpayer appealed the town's assessment on her home of $54,400 (land, $17,800; buildings, $35,600). The taxpayer cited several arguments including:

1. errors in the property record card;
2. the failure of the town to grant an exemption;

3. her inability to pay due to her disability;

4. the poor shape of the access road to her property.

Appeal board decision.   Against the taxpayer, except the town was ordered to correct any deficiencies recorded on the property record card.

Main issues involved.   Whether or not the property was disproportionately assessed because of the reasons cited by the taxpayer.

Comments.   The board decided that there was an error made by the assessor regarding the land size of the property, which it ordered corrected. Although the appeal only applied to tax year 1989, the board reminded the town that the board had the power "... on its own initiative, after receiving information, to review an improper assessment even if the taxpayer has not filed an appeal." In other words, the board felt the town should take steps to ensure that the land measurement error was corrected for all future tax bills. It informed the town that it would check to see if it had done so, even if the taxpayer filed no other appeals.

The taxpayer cited other property record card errors. However, the board noted that "... the taxpayer did *not* allow the town into her home to gather the information needed to accurately complete the card. While her refusal cannot be grounds for dismissing her appeal...her continued refusal will keep the town from determining whether errors in the card exist." The board indicated further that such refusal might weigh against future appeals by the taxpayer.

Regarding the taxpayer's other assertions (#2–4 above), the taxpayer failed to prove her case to the satisfaction of the board.

Case 4: New Hampshire BTLA Docket #5900-89 _____

Fact summary.   The taxpayers appealed the town's assessed value of $24,850 (land, $18,950, buildings, $5000) based on the following contentions:

1. a neighbor has 67 acres of "better" land assessed at $30,850, compared with their 24.5 acres;

2. the land is only accessible in the summertime and is used as a camp;

3. the property lacks a septic system and has an outhouse;

4. because of limited frontage, the property cannot be subdivided without putting in another road.

The town argued the assessment was proper because:

1. the property consists of two sites, and adjustments to their assessed values were made for size and topography;

2. an insulated garage was added to the property, which was later utilized as a camp;

3. the property was given a 15 percent site adjustment, and an additional 50 percent adjustment for the condition of the access;

4. the assessment is consistent with other lots.

Appeal board decision. Taxpayers' appeal denied.

Main issues involved. Whether or not the taxpayers had satisfied the burden of proof in showing the assessment to be disproportionate to similar properties.

Comments. While some of the taxpayers' arguments have merit, others are weak. For example, neighboring properties are also used as summertime camps, so this in itself, is not exceptional enough to lower the value of the property. Primarily, however, the town was able to show that it had already made adjustments to the property's value for the poor access and lack of frontage. It was also able to demonstrate conclusively that the assessment was consistent with that of similar properties.

Remember, the burden of proof requires a taxpayer's evidence to be clearly superior to that of the municipality. If both sides have similar arguments, the municipality will win.

Case 5: New Hampshire BTLA Docket #5929-89

Fact summary. The taxpayer appealed the town's assessment of $24,000 on a 0.34-acre lot. The lot possessed undesirable topography and was not zoned as a buildable lot. The taxpayer argued that:

1. The property has no access to a paved street.
2. Access is over a dirt road.
3. The land was purchased several years earlier for $6400;
4. A recent appraisal indicated a value of $11,000.

The town argued that:

1. Adjustments were made for topography and lack of frontage
2. The value was supported by comparable sales.

Appeal board decision. In favor of the taxpayer, although the amount of the abatement was not the complete amount requested by the taxpayer.

Main issues involved. (1) Whether or not the town used proper comparable properties to determine value, and; (2) whether or not the effects of zoning regulations were properly accounted for by the town.

Comments. The board rightly decided that the town's choices of comparable property sales were inappropriate since they were "...all developed parcels with direct road frontage on a paved street." The town was therefore attempting to compare more valuable *sites* with superior locations to less valuable raw land. Secondly, since a variance would be required to the zoning in order to build on the lot, it was not appropriate for the town to value the lot as if it was already zoned for such.

The board's decision resulted in a new finding of value that was somewhere between the figures offered by the taxpayer and the town. This illustrates the fact that boards are empowered to arrive at their own conclusions of value, and often do so. They are not simply required to choose one side's opinion over another.

Case 6: New Hampshire BTLA Docket #6397-89 _____

Fact summary. The taxpayers appealed an assessment on a mobile home and lot of $37,050 (land, $21,550; building, $15,500). They argued that the home was merely a stripped shell that was hauled away at a cost of $1500, subsequent to the assessment date. They offered a demolition permit obtained from the town as evidence.

The town argued that the assessment on the building was within an acceptable statistical deviation from assessments on similar mobile homes.

Appeal board decision. In favor of the taxpayer. The board pointed out that the town's statistics were meaningless in this case. "The change in the status of the mobile home from a habitable residence connected to public utilities...to a stripped shell waiting to be removed...is a significant enough change not to be overlooked and explained away in the morass of statistical analyses."

Main issues involved. Whether or not an assessment is equitable merely because it falls within an allowable statistical deviation from assessments of similar properties.

Comments. The board rightly decided that the particular facts of this case did not support reliance upon the town's statistical justification for the assessment.

Case 7: New Hampshire BTLA Docket #0127-89 _____

Fact summary. The board was asked to rule upon the validity of a town wide revaluation of properties that it had earlier ordered performed. A group of taxpayers had protested the accuracy of the revaluation, citing several examples of individual assessments that they considered inaccurate.

Appeal board decision. In favor of the town, ruling that the revaluation had been performed with an acceptable degree of accuracy.

Main issues involved. Whether or not a small percentage of inaccurate assessments invalidated a mass appraisal of properties in a town.

Comments. The board reasonably ruled that the proper forum for the small number of inaccurate assessments demonstrated by the taxpayers was the normal appeal process. The board indicated it would require "... conclusive evidence of widespread inequities..." in order to justify ordering another townwide revaluation.

Homeowner and taxpayer associations take note. If you choose to challenge the validity of an entire revaluation of properties in your area, your evidence will need to be especially compelling. In particular, it must demonstrate a widespread pattern of assessing inaccuracy.

Case 8: New Hampshire BTLA Docket #4287-88

Fact summary. A taxpayer appealed the assessment of several other taxpayers' properties, which is allowed under New Hampshire state law. He claimed the assessments were too low. The taxpayers, in turn, objected to the appeal on the grounds that the complainant had not appealed the assessments of all properties in the town that were assessed too low. They claimed discrimination for this reason.

Appeal board decision. In favor of the taxpayer bringing the appeal.

Main issues involved. Whether or not the taxpayers were discriminated against by being singled out by another taxpayer for an appeal of their assessments.

Comments. The objection to the appeal failed, simply because such appeals are allowed by New Hampshire state law.

It is possible in some states for third party taxpayers to become involved in appeals of another taxpayer's property assessment. The lesson here is to know who may appeal an assessment where you live. (We might add also, don't give your neighbors reason to challenge your assessment for you!)

Case 9: New Hampshire BTLA Docket #6076-89

Fact summary. The taxpayer's estate appealed the assessment of $98,700 on the property (land, $62,800; buildings, $35,900). The administrator of the estate argued that a fire had substantially damaged the buildings, offering as evidence an insurance company statement that the buildings had been totally destroyed.

The town argued that some portions of the buildings were still useable, even though there was substantial fire and smoke damage.

Appeal board decision. In favor of the estate, but not for the full amount requested. The board found that even though the damage was, in fact, very extensive, some of the structural remains had salvage value.

Main issues involved. Whether a proper determination of the value of the remaining portion of the fire damaged buildings had been made by the town.

Comments. This case demonstrates two points. First, even a building reduced to a pile of rubble may have some salvage value as scrap. Secondly, appeal boards will often determine a value which differs from those offered by other parties to the appeal.

Case 10: New Hampshire BTLA Docket #6674-89

Fact summary. The city appealed to the board for a rehearing of a previous case which it had lost. The city cited previously unsubmitted evidence which it felt would result in the board's earlier decision being overturned.

Appeal board decision. Request for a rehearing denied.

Main issues involved. Whether or not it is proper to request a rehearing based on previously unsubmitted evidence that could have been presented in the original appeal.

Comments. This case has bearing on similar cases in other jurisdictions. Many boards will not allow previously unsubmitted evidence to be presented if it could have been presented earlier, as in this case. Boards will make limited exceptions for evidence that was not available by any means earlier, but, that later became available. Also, they may be more receptive to receiving later evidence if a request for a delay in the hearing has been made, pending the availability of required evidence.

Case 11: New Hampshire BTLA Docket #6674-89

Fact summary. This was an appeal from the city's denial of the taxpayers' request for an abatement of interest paid, as a result of the late payment of their tax bill. The basis of their appeal was that the tax bill had been incorrectly sent to the previous owner. They therefore felt they were not notified of the taxes due, as required by law, and were not responsible for the late payment.

Appeal board decision. In favor of the taxpayers.

Main issues involved. (1) Whether or not the city fulfilled its duty of giving legal notice of the tax assessment by sending the bill to the previous owners, and; (2) whether the city's administration of other state property-tax laws was adequate.

Comments. Although this case encompassed a number of issues, the board was primarily concerned with the city's failure to comply with the letter and the spirit of various state property-tax laws. The board was particularly critical of the city in its written decision, citing "... City officials who are either uninformed or who simply choose not to follow the law."

This case demonstrates the importance of awareness of local and state property-tax law in regards to legal assessing errors.

Case 12: New Hampshire BTLA Docket #6307-89

Fact summary. The taxpayer appealed the town's assessment of $50,400 (land, $17,300; buildings, $33,100). The property consisted of several old buildings "grandfathered" for commercial use in a residentially zoned rural area. The buildings were largely abandoned and no longer used for commercial purposes. The land was partially swampy and generally of poor quality.

Appeal board decision. In favor of the taxpayer.

Main issues involved. Whether the town had considered the degree of functional depreciation of the buildings that was present.

Comments. The board decided that a 70 percent functional depreciation factor should be applied to the buildings, resulting in a new assessment for the buildings of $9950. This was a case of the town wanting to have its cake and eat it too. Even though the buildings were no longer being used for commercial purposes, the town assessed them as if commercially viable and did not adequately account for the large amount of functional depreciation present.

Case 13: New Hampshire BTLA Docket #7105-89

Fact summary. The taxpayers appealed the town's assessment on their home of $151,000 (land, $42,300; building, $108,700). They argued that, based on a comparison of their home with sales of neighboring homes, the assessment was excessive.

Appeal board decision. In favor of the taxpayers.

Main issues involved. Whether or not the town had properly considered the sales value of neighboring properties in assessing the subject home.

Comments. This is a good example of a case which relied, primarily, upon the comparable sales approach to value. In particular, the taxpayers successfully argued that the town had not made proper adjustments to the value of comparable properties in assessing the taxpayers' home. They were able to cite differences in the view from their property, the quality of their land, the condition of the access road to their property and general sales data for the neighborhood in convincing the board. The case was won on the basis of the quality and quantity of the taxpayers' evidence.

For a similar case with the opposite result, see the next example.

Case 14: New Hampshire BTLA Docket #6188-89

Fact summary. The taxpayer appealed the assessment on his home of $567,700 (land, $323,400; building, $244,300). He cited two sales of neighboring properties as evidence of the disproportionate assessment. The town used other property sales as evidence supporting the assessment.

Appeal board decision.   In favor of the town.

Main issues involved.   Whether the taxpayer's comparable sales approach to value truly reflected the value of his property or whether the town's assessment was proper.

Comments.   The taxpayer lost this case because he did not make adjustments to the sales prices of the comparable homes as required when using this approach to value. The town's comparable sales analysis was more thorough. It made adjustments to the sales prices of comparable homes for such factors as the time of the sale, the value of site preparation, and the availability of certain utilities.

11

California–A Unique Case

In general, the art of government consists in taking as much money as possible from one party of the citizens to give to the other.
VOLTAIRE (1694–1778),
French philosopher and writer

California deserves mention in its own chapter for two reasons. First, as a result of Proposition 13, California is unique among the 50 states for the manner in which property is assessed for tax purposes. Secondly, as the state in which the tax revolt first began in America, its experiences may offer insight into the future of property taxation in the rest of the country.

Proposition 13

On June 6, 1978 a large majority of California voters approved Proposition 13, which added Article XIII A to the state constitution. Several later amendments have modified it somewhat, but Proposition 13 has maintained three primary features:

1. Property taxes on most classes of real property, including residential properties, are limited to 1 percent of taxable value, plus any additional yearly amounts necessary to pay off "voter approved" indebtedness.

2. Real property must be valued at fair market value as of the 1975 assessment year, or as of the date that the property changed ownership if later, or as of the date that the property was newly constructed if later. If a portion of the property has been newly constructed, only the new portion is valued as of the date of completion. (The yearly assessment date for California is March 1, and is known as the *lien date*.)

3. Once a lien date is determined for a property (either in 1975 or in a later year), assessed property values may not increase more than 2 percent per year. (They may increase less than 2 percent and they are not limited in the amount of possible decrease.) The increase or decrease to value is a factor of the inflation rate for the year, and other economic and physical influences.

Proposition 13 was a popular reaction to, what many perceived to be, government inability and unwillingness to overhaul the property tax system. California property taxes prior to the amendment were among the highest in the country, and politicians were unable to wean themselves from a semmingly endless supply of property-tax revenue.

Proposition 13 was effective in reducing property taxes. The California Taxpayers' Association estimated that $228 billion in property-tax savings occurred during the first decade the amendment was implemented. Proposition 13 also sparked interest and support among taxpayers in other states for various types of legislative controls on the taxation of property. Since 1978, a majority of states have enacted or considered laws limiting property taxes in some fashion.

The amendment proved to be a two-edged sword for Californians, however, since many services were cut, and needed-work to the infrastructure of roads, bridges, and other municipal structures was deferred. By one estimate, Californians will need to spend $90 billion by the end of the century to upgrade and expand its municipal infrastructure. To make up some of the revenue lost from property taxation, various kinds of user fees and taxes have been implemented. The net result is a lessening of California's dependence on property-tax revenues, and an increase in its dependence on other sources of income.

As time marches forward from the base assessment year of 1975, it becomes more and more obvious that Proposition 13 has resulted in some gross inequities in property-tax assessment in California. If you owned your home since 1975 for instance, the yearly increases to its assessed value has been minimal (2 percent maximum per year), based on the limitations of Proposition 13. Your neighbor, living in a recently purchased, and nearly identical home, could be faced with a much higher assessed value, since the new purchase would trigger a reassessment to full current market value.

While everyone pays only 1 percent of assessed value each year (more if specifically approved by voters), not every property in a class is assessed at the same percentage of current fair market value, which is the desired norm elsewhere in the country. Proposition 13 has helped create a caste system of sorts among property owners in California—those who enjoy a low assessment by virtue of long-time ownership and those whose taxes are based on full market value simply because they recently purchased their home.

Personal property is not covered under the provisions of Proposition 13 and, thus, remains taxable at fair market value as of the most recent lien date. Household goods and personal effects are, however, fully exempted from taxation. Proposition 13 did not, in any way, affect the granting or denying of the numerous real- and personal-property tax exemptions available in California.

Appealing a Property-Tax Assessment in California

If you pursue an appeal of the assessment on your California house or condominium, you must prove that the assessed value is higher than it should be, considering the particular lien date on which your assessment is based. The relative fairness or equity of your property assessment compared with similar properties is not pertinent if the other properties are assessed at fair market value as of different lien dates than your property.

Increases in assessed value, greater than 2 percent per year, that are due to ownership transfer or new construction, are subject to *supplemental assessments* in California.

Supplemental assessments are computed by the assessor and are detailed on the Notice of Changed Assessment that the property owner will receive. The following example illustrates how the supplemental assessment and supplemental property taxes are computed on a newly purchased home.

New base-year value as result of sale	$275,000
Taxable value prior to sale	− $145,000
Supplemental assessment	$130,000
Multiplied by new tax rate	× 0.0112
Supplemental taxes	$ 1,456

In this example, the new owner will pay $1456 of supplemental taxes which are in addition to the taxes on the base assessed value of $145,000. The supplemental taxes are paid one time only. They are prorated from the date of ownership change or new construction, so they will not always be for a full year. The total taxes due in this example are $3080:

$$\$275,000 \times 0.0112 = \$3080$$

In preparing an appeal of an assessment in California, you should verify that your property's lien date is correct. Your property's lien date may have been incorrectly changed by the assessor, resulting in an unnecessarily high assessment. If you can show that your property's lien date should be earlier than the assessor says it is, you may qualify for a lower property assessment. Although an assessor may change the lien date from 1975 to a later year based on change of ownership or new construction, there are exceptions to both of these instances. Consider the following points as they may apply to your property.

Change of ownership

The meaning of "change of ownership" appears, at first, to be obvious, but in fact, there are many fine shades of distinction in California law. While it is beyond the scope of this book to discuss them all, California excepts many types of ownership transfers from triggering a change in lien dates. Some examples of exceptions include:

- Interspousal transfers, such as those that might result from divorce or death of one of the spouses.
- Transfers between parents and children of the principal place of residence, up to a maximum of $1,000,000 assessed value.
- Foreclosures (under certain conditions).

- Transfers resulting from a tax delinquency.
- Transfers between or among affiliated corporations.
- Transfers resulting from the addition or deletion of partners in a continuing partnership.
- Refinancing of an existing mortgage.

New construction

New construction for matters of property taxation in California means "...any substantial addition to land or improvements such as adding land fill, retaining walls, curbs, gutters or sewers, or constructing a new building or changing an existing improvement so as to add horizontally or vertically to its square footage..."* New construction may refer to an entire property or just a portion of it, as, for example, an addition on a house. Significant upgrading or remodeling of a home may be sufficient to qualify as new construction, although each case must be considered individually. The following are not considered new construction:

- Normal repair and maintenance, such as painting, replacement of a roof, or installation of vinyl siding.
- Property destroyed completely or partially by a natural disaster, which is reconstructed in a timely manner and which is substantially equivalent in value to the property it replaces. "Substantially equivalent" is the key criteria which the assessor uses to decide the issue in this kind of case.
- A house which is newly constructed for resale purposes. The builder must apply for a builder's exclusion in order to defer the supplemental assessment. The supplemental assessment will occur when the new owner purchases the home.

When a building permit is issued in California, the county assessor receives a copy and uses it to determine if the planned work will qualify as new construction.

In cases where a supplemental assessment is triggered by partial new construction of an existing property, homeowners should carefully review exactly what is being assessed as new construction. It is possible, for example, that the assessor has listed three rooms as being newly constructed when actually only one room was.

For a more in depth explanation of how both change of ownership and new construction are interpreted in California, as well as the latest changes to state property taxation laws, contact your local county assessor. Specific application procedures, deadlines, and other guidance in the preparation of property-tax appeals is available there as well.

Property Tax Facts for Policy Makers Pamphlet No. 29, California State Board of Equalization, Sacramento, CA, August 1987.

If satisfied that the lien date for your property is correct, the next step in preparing an appeal of your assessment is to formulate your own opinion of value for the property. This is done using the comparable sales and cost approaches to value, as discussed elsewhere in this book. Both are accepted methods in California.

When using the comparable sales approach, find other homes that have been reassessed in the same general time period as your property was (as of a lien date that is close to your property's.) Remember, the sale of each comparable property will trigger a new lien date for the property. If similar lien dates are used, the sales value of the comparables will relate more closely to the assessed value of your property.

With the exception of the items mentioned above that are specific to California, your appeal of a California property assessment can follow the steps we recommend in Chap. 8, "Organizing Your Tax Appeal."

In summary then, you should do the following when appealing a property-tax assessment in California:

1. Determine the amount of the assessment, including supplemental assessments.

2. Determine if your property has been assessed as of the correct lien date. If the lien date has changed due to change of ownership or new construction, verify that the assessor has properly applied these reasons for making the change. It is possible that your property's lien date should not have changed at all.

3. Estimate your own opinion of value based on the comparable sales and cost approaches to value. When using the comparable sales approach, use comparable properties with sale dates (and therefore lien dates) similar to your own property's lien date.

4. Adhere to all procedural rules and deadlines in filing your appeal.

5. Consider all other factors detailed in Chap. 8, "Organizing Your Tax Appeal" that may apply to your appeal.

The Future of the Tax Revolt

Proposition 13 has, so far, survived more or less intact. It is becoming increasingly likely, however, that it may eventually succumb to a Supreme Court challenge, or be replaced by the state legislature with another, more equitable law. In fact, the Supreme Court has already agreed to hear one challenge to the law.

A counter movement is shaping up in California that seeks to undo some of the fiscal constrictions that Proposition 13 placed on the state. Whatever the future may hold for California, it is clear that the after shocks of Proposition 13 will continue to be felt around the nation.

What are the lessons to be learned by the rest of the country from California's unique property-tax experiences? Clearly, limitations on property taxes are popular, but service cutbacks are not. More and more, voters seem willing to accept other kinds of taxes and user fees in lieu of property taxes, if they are earmarked for a specific purpose. Rather than grant politicians a blank check, voters would prefer to control the purse strings themselves as much as possible. Governments will always need money, but how they get it and where they spend it will continue to evolve.

However, it is unlikely that the basic concept of ad valorem taxation will change very much. Although various schemes will continue to emerge to control and limit property taxes, our country will probably always depend on them. The basic methods of valuing and assessing property for tax purposes will continue to be used. Inequitable assessments will continue to occur. In the end, property owners, like yourself, will still need to monitor property assessments to be assured of fair and equitable treatment.

Individual State Information

Information contained in this appendix is accurate to the best of our knowledge as of the publication date. However, it is subject to change. Therefore, for the very latest rules, procedures, and laws regarding property taxation in your state, contact your local assessor or the departments listed here.

ALABAMA

Agency Name: State Board of Revenue
    Ad Valorem Tax Division
    50 Ripley Street
    Montgomery, AL 36132
    Telephone #1: (205)242-1525
Assessment Date: October 1
Notification Date: May 15 (may vary by locality)
Tax Bill Payment Date: October 1; December 31
Appeal Grievance Period: 10 days after notification date
Revaluation Period: Varies
Personal Property Tax? Yes
Homestead Exemption? Yes

PROPERTY TAX APPEAL LEVELS

Level 1: Informal meeting with assessor
Level 2: Circuit Court
Level 3: State Supreme Court

Notes: Any authorized agent may represent a taxpayer in appeal proceedings.

ALASKA

Agency Name: State Assessor
    Department of Community &
        Regional Affairs
    P.O. Box BH
    Juneau, AK 99811
Telephone #1: (907)465-4787
Telephone #2: (907)465-4750
Assessment Date: January 1

Notification Date: Varies between January 1 and May 1
Tax Bill Payment Date: Bills mailed by July, paymentdates vary
Appeal Grievance Period: 30 days from date of mailing
Revaluation Period: Not specified in state statutes
Personal Property Tax? Yes, but varies by municipality
Homestead Exemption? Yes, at option of each municipality

PROPERTY TAX APPEAL LEVELS

Level 1: Informal meeting with assessor
Level 2: Local Board of Equalization
Level 3: Alaska Superior Court
Level 4: Alaska Supreme Court

Notes: A taxpayer may designate any person as a representative in a property-tax appeal.

ARIZONA

Agency Name: Arizona Department of Revenue
    Division of Property Valuation
    1600 W. Monroe Street, 8th Floor
    Phoenix, AZ 85007
Telephone #1: (602)542-3529
Assessment Date: January 1
Notification Date: November 15
Tax Bill Payment Date: 1st half—October 1, 2nd half—March 1

Appeal Grievance Period: Through January 15
(January 1 for 1993 and thereafter)
Revaluation Period: Varies
Personal Property Tax? Yes
Homestead Exemption? No

PROPERTY TAX APPEAL LEVELS

Level 1: County Assessor
Level 2: County Board of Equalization
Level 3: State Board of Tax Appeals
Level 4: Tax Court

Notes: Any authorized agent may represent a tax-payer in appeal proceedings for Levels 1 and 2. Arizona tax statutes may be found in Title 42 of Arizona Revised Statutes.

ARKANSAS

Agency Name: Public Service Commission
Assessment Coordination Division
1614 West Third Street
Little Rock, AR 72201
Telephone #1: (501)324-9240
Assessment Date: January 1
Notification Date: By 3rd Monday in August
Tax Bill Payment Date: 3rd Monday of Feb., Apr., & Jul.
Appeal Grievance Period: August 1 through October 1
Revaluation Period: Varies
Personal Property Tax? Yes
Homestead Exemption? Yes, for low income elderly

PROPERTY TAX APPEAL LEVELS

Level 1: Informal meeting with assessor
Level 2: County Board of Equalization
Level 3: County Court
Level 4: Circuit Court
Level 5: Supreme Court

Notes: Any authorized agent may represent a tax-payer in appeal proceedings.

CALIFORNIA

Agency Name: California Board of Equalization
Department of Property Taxes
Assessment Standards Division
1719 24th Street
Sacramento, CA 95816
Telephone #1: (916)445-4982
Assessment Date: March 1
Notification Date: Varies by county
Tax Bill Payment Date: December 10; April 10
Appeal Grievance Period: July 2 through September 5
Revaluation Period: 1 Year
Personal Property Tax? Yes
Homestead Exemption? Yes

PROPERTY TAX APPEAL LEVELS

Level 1: Informal meeting with assessor
Level 2: Board of Assessment Appeals
Level 3: Superior Court
Level 4: Supreme Court

Notes: See Chap. 11 for more information about California property taxation.

COLORADO

Agency Name: Colorado Department of Local Affairs
Division of Property Taxation
1313 Sherman Street
Room 419
Denver, CO 80203
Telephone #1: (303)866-2371
Assessment Date: January 1
Notification Date: May 1 (real property); June 15 (personal property)
Tax Bill Payment Date: After 1st of year
Appeal Grievance Period: May 1 through June 15 (real property)
Revaluation Period: Every odd numbered year
Personal Property Tax? Yes
Homestead Exemption? No

PROPERTY TAX APPEAL LEVELS

Level 1: Informal meeting with assessor
Level 2: County Board of Equalization
Level 3: State Board of Assessment
Level 4: District Court or Binding Arbitration
Level 5: Court of Appeals
Level 6: Supreme Court

Notes: Taxpayers must give written authorization to persons representing them, such as property-tax consultants.

CONNECTICUT

Agency Name: State of Connecticut
Office of Policy & Management
Intergovernmental Relations
Division
80 Washington Street
Hartford, CT 06106
Telephone #1: (203)566-8170
Assessment Date: October 1
Notification Date: January 31
Tax Bill Payment Date: July 1 (May vary by county)
Appeal Grievance Period: Varies (Usually in February)
Revaluation Period: 10 years
Personal Property Tax? Yes
Homestead Exemption? Yes

PROPERTY TAX APPEAL LEVELS

Level 1: Informal meeting with assessor
Level 2: Board of Tax Review
Level 3: Superior Court

DELAWARE

Agency Name: Director
New Castle County Department of Finance
820 North French Street
Wilmington, DE 18901
Telephone #1: (302)577-3315
Assessment Date: July 1 (may vary by county)
Notification Date: 30 days prior to tax bill
Tax Bill Payment Date: October 1
Appeal Grievance Period: March 15
Revaluation Period: Varies
Personal Property Tax? No
Homestead Exemption? Yes

PROPERTY TAX APPEAL LEVELS

Level 1: Informal meeting with assessor
Level 2: Department of Finance of Board of Assessment
Level 3: Superior Court
Level 4: Supreme Court

Notes: Contact each county's Department of Finance for individual county information: Kent County—414 Federal St. P.O. Box 802 Dover, DE 19903-0802; Sussex County—Georgetown, DE 19947.

DISTRICT OF COLUMBIA

Agency Name: Real Property Assessments
300 Indiana Avenue, N.W.
Room 2115
Washington, DC 20001
Telephone #1: (202)727-6460
Assessment Date: January 1
Notification Date: February 28
Tax Bill Payment Date: March 31; September 15
Appeal Grievance Period: April 15 deadline
Revaluation Period: 1 year
Personal Property Tax? Yes
Homestead Exemption? Yes

PROPERTY TAX APPEAL LEVELS

Level 1: Informal meeting with assessor
Level 2: Superior Court

FLORIDA

Agency Name: Florida Department of Revenue
Division of Ad Valorem Tax
Woodcrest Office Building
P.O. Box 3000
Tallahassee, FL 32315-3000
Telephone #1: (904)487-3595
Telephone #2: (904)488-3338
Assessment Date: January 1
Notification Date: Varies by county
Tax Bill Payment Date: April 1
Appeal Grievance Period: Varies by county
Revaluation Period: 1 year
Personal Property Tax? Yes
Homestead Exemption? Yes

PROPERTY TAX APPEAL LEVELS

Level 1: Informal meeting with assessor
Level 2: Property Appraiser
Level 3: Property Appraisal Adjustment Board
Level 4: Board to the Circuit Court
Level 5: State Supreme Court

Notes: Any designated person may represent a taxpayer in tax appeals. Contact Tax Watch, Inc. 1114 T-Ville Rd. Tallahassee, FL for additional information on property tax matters.

GEORGIA

Agency Name: Georgia Department of Revenue
Property Tax Division
405 Trinity-Washington Building
Atlanta, GA 30334
Telephone #1: (404)656-4108
Telephone #2: (404)656-4109
Assessment Date: January 1
Notification Date: Varies
Tax Bill Payment Date: Varies
Appeal Grievance Period: Varies
Revaluation Period: Varies
Personal Property Tax? Yes
Homestead Exemption? Yes

PROPERTY TAX APPEAL LEVELS

Level 1: Informal meeting with assessor
Level 2: County Board of Tax Assessors
Level 3: County Board of Equalization
Level 4: Superior Court
Level 5: State Supreme Court

Notes: Taxpayer may be represented by any designated person in a property-tax appeal.

HAWAII

Agency Name: Dept. of Finance, City & County
of Honolulu
Real Property Division
842 Bethel Street, 2nd Floor
Honolulu, HI 96813
Telephone #1: (808)527-5500
Telephone #2: (808)527-5507
Assessment Date: January 1
Notification Date: March 15
Tax Bill Payment Date: August 20; February 20
Appeal Grievance Period: March 15 through
April 9
Revaluation Period: Annually
Personal Property Tax? No
Homestead Exemption?

PROPERTY TAX APPEAL LEVELS

Level 1: Informal meeting with assessor
Level 2: County Assessor
Level 3: District Board of Review
Level 4: Tax Appeal Court
Level 5: State Supreme Court

Notes: Information shown is for City and County of Honolulu. Contact Maui, Hawaii, or Kauai county assessing departments for specific dates and procedures in those counties.

IDAHO

Agency Name: State of Idaho State Tax
Commission
Personal Property Bureau
700 West State Street
P.O. Box 36
Boise, ID 83722
Telephone #1: (208)334-7733
Telephone #2: (208)334-0320
Assessment Date: January 1
Notification Date: 1st Monday in June
Tax Bill Payment Date: December 20; June 20
Appeal Grievance Period: 4th Monday in June
through 1st Monday in November
Revaluation Period: 5 years, 20% of all properties reappraised annually
Personal Property Tax? Yes
Homestead Exemption? Yes

PROPERTY TAX APPEAL LEVELS

Level 1: Informal meeting with assessor
Level 2: County Assessor
Level 3: County Board of Equalization or State
Courts
Level 4: State Board of Tax Appeals
Level 5: State Board to the District Court
Level 6: State Supreme Court

Notes: There are some restrictions on who may represent a taxpayer at appeals, depending upon the level of appeal.

ILLINOIS

Agency Name: Illinois Property Tax Appeal
Board
404 Stratton Building
P.O. Box 19278
Springfield, IL 67964-9278
Telephone #1: (217)782-6076
Assessment Date: January 1
Notification Date: Varies
Tax Bill Payment Date: June 1; September 1
(varies by county)
Appeal Grievance Period: 30 days from notification
Revaluation Period: Usually 4 years, varies by
county
Personal Property Tax? No
Homestead Exemption? Yes

PROPERTY TAX APPEAL LEVELS

Level 1: Informal meeting with assessor

Level 2: County Board of Review (except Cook County)
Level 3: State Property Tax Appeal Board
Level 4: Circuit Court
Level 5: Superior Court

Notes: Taxpayers may be represented by themselves or an Illinois attorney. Other parties such as consultants, appraisers, etc. may offer testimony, but may not directly represent taxpayer at appeals.

INDIANA

Agency Name: State of Indiana
State Board of Tax
Commissioners
201 State Office Building
Indianapolis, IN 46204
Telephone #1: (317)232-3761
Assessment Date: March 1
Notification Date: Varies, but is date of mailing of notice of assessment
Tax Bill Payment Date: May 10; November 10
Appeal Grievance Period: 30 days from date of mailing of notice of tax
Revaluation Period: 4 years
Personal Property Tax? Yes
Homestead Exemption? Yes

PROPERTY TAX APPEAL LEVELS

Level 1: Informal meeting with assessor
Level 2: County Board of Review
Level 3: State Board of Tax Commissioners
Level 4: Indiana Tax Court
Level 5: State Supreme Court

Notes: A taxpayer may be represented by a property-tax consultant at either the County Board of Review or the State Board of Tax Commissioners, but not at any level of the court system.

IOWA

Agency Name: Iowa Department of Revenue & Finance
Local Government Services Division
Hoover State Office Building
Des Moines, IA 50319
Telephone #1: (515)281-4040
Assessment Date: January 1
Notification Date: April 15
Tax Bill Payment Date: September 30; March 31
Appeal Grievance Period: April 16 through May 5

Revaluation Period: 2 years
Personal Property Tax? No
Homestead Exemption? Yes

PROPERTY TAX APPEAL LEVELS

Level 1: Informal meeting with assessor
Level 2: Board of Review
Level 3: District Court of the County
Level 4: State Supreme Court

Notes: Any authorized agent may act on behalf of taxpayer in appeal proceedings.

KANSAS

Agency Name: Kansas Department of Revenue
Division of Property Valuation
Robert B. Docking State Office Building
526 South
Topeka, KS 66612-1585
Telephone #1: (913)296-2365
Assessment Date: January 1
Notification Date: Between January 1 and March 1
Tax Bill Payment Date: December 20; June 20
Appeal Grievance Period: 21 days from notification
Revaluation Period: 1 year
Personal Property Tax? Yes
Homestead Exemption? No

PROPERTY TAX APPEAL LEVELS

Level 1: Informal meeting with assessor
Level 2: County Board of Equalization
Level 3: State Board of Tax Appeals
Level 4: District Court
Level 5: State Supreme Court

Notes: Property tax consultants may represent a taxpayer at the county level of appeal. At higher levels, a taxpayer must be self-represented or represented by an attorney.

KENTUCKY

Agency Name: Commonwealth of Kentucky
Department of Property Tax
Revenue Cabinet
592 East Main Street
Frankfort, KY 40620
Telephone #1: (502)564-8338
Assessment Date: January 1
Notification Date: March 1

Tax Bill Payment Date: November 1 (Discount); November 2 (No discount)

Appeal Grievance Period: 45 days from notification

Revaluation Period: Annually

Personal Property Tax? Yes

Homestead Exemption? Yes

PROPERTY TAX APPEAL LEVELS

Level 1: Informal meeting with assessor
Level 2: Local Board of Tax Appeals
Level 3: Kentucky Board of Tax Appeals
Level 4: Circuit Court
Level 5: Court of Appeals

Notes: There are no restrictions on who may represent a taxpayer in appeal proceedings. Personal property tax returns are always due by April 15.

LOUISIANA

Agency Name: Louisiana Tax Commission
Property Tax Division
923 Executive Park Avenue
Suite 12
Baton Rouge, LA 70806

Telephone #1: (504)925-7830

Assessment Date: January 1

Notification Date: Not prescribed by state law

Tax Bill Payment Date: December 31

Appeal Grievance Period: August 1 through August 15 (may vary by parish)

Revaluation Period: 4 years real property, annually personal property

Personal Property Tax? Yes

Homestead Exemption? Yes

PROPERTY TAX APPEAL LEVELS

Level 1: Informal meeting with assessor
Level 2: Board of Review (Parish Governing Authority)
Level 3: Louisiana Tax Commission
Level 4: District Court
Level 5: Circuit Court
Level 6: Supreme Court

Notes: There is no requirement that a taxpayer be notified of an assessment, although several parishes do so.

MAINE

Agency Name: Bureau of Taxation
State Office Building
Augusta, ME 04333

Telephone #1: (207)289-2011

Assessment Date: Varies by municipality

Notification Date: Varies by municipality

Tax Bill Payment Date: Varies by municipality

Appeal Grievance Period: 6 months for valuation errors, 3 years for

Revaluation Period: Varies by municipality

Personal Property Tax? Yes

Homestead Exemption? No

PROPERTY TAX APPEAL LEVELS

Level 1: Informal meeting with assessor
Level 2: Local Board or County Commissioners
Level 3: Superior Court
Level 4: State Board of Property Tax Review

MARYLAND

Agency Name: State Department of Assessment & Taxation
301 West Preston Street
Baltimore, MD 21201

Telephone #1: (301)225-1191

Assessment Date: January 1

Notification Date: 1st or 2nd week in December

Tax Bill Payment Date: September 30

Appeal Grievance Period: 45 days after notice

Revaluation Period: 3 years

Personal Property Tax? Yes

Homestead Exemption? Yes

PROPERTY TAX APPEAL LEVELS

Level 1: Informal meeting with assessor
Level 2: Assessment Appeal Board
Level 3: Tax Court
Level 4: Circuit Court
Level 5: Court of Special Appeals
Level 6: Court of Appeals

Notes: Contact the Homeowner's Tax Credit Program, 105 West Christopher Avenue, Room 303 Towson, MD 21204 or 1-800-492-3790 (toll-free in Maryland) for other property tax information.

MASSACHUSETTS

Agency Name: Commonwealth of Massachusetts
Department of Revenue
Division of Local Services
200 Portland Street
Boston, MA 02114-1715

Telephone #1: (617)727-2300

Telephone #2: (617)727-4217
Assessment Date: January 1
Notification Date: Varies by county
Tax Bill Payment Date: August 1; November 1 (quarterly in some towns)
Appeal Grievance Period: Within 30 days after actual tax bill is sent
Revaluation Period: 3 years
Personal Property Tax? Yes
Homestead Exemption? No

PROPERTY TAX APPEAL LEVELS

Level 1: Informal meeting with assessor
Level 2: County Commissioner
Level 3: Appellate Tax Court
Level 4: Appeals Court
Level 5: State Supreme Court

Notes: Many towns and cities issue estimated tax bills prior to actual bills. The 30-day period for filing abatement or exemption applications runs from the date the actual (not estimated) bills are mailed.

MICHIGAN

Agency Name: Department of Treasury
Property Tax Division
430 West Allegan
4th Floor, Treasury Building
Lansing, MI 48922
Telephone #1: (517)373-0500
Telephone #2: (517)373-0501
Assessment Date: December 31
Notification Date: 10 days before Board of Review (last week in February)
Tax Bill Payment Date: Varies by county
Appeal Grievance Period: (Local Board) 2nd Monday in March through
Revaluation Period: 1 year
Personal Property Tax? Yes
Homestead Exemption? Real property—no; personal property—yes

PROPERTY TAX APPEAL LEVELS

Level 1: Informal meeting with assessor
Level 2: City (Local) Board of Review
Level 3: Michigan Tax Tribunal

Notes: Contact Michigan Consumer's Council, 414 Hollister Building, Lansing, MI 48933, Tel:(517)373-0947 for copy of brochure, "How to Review & Appeal Your Property Tax Assessment."

MINNESOTA

Agency Name: State of Minnesota
Local Government Services
Division
Mail Station 3340
St. Paul, MN 55146-3340
Telephone #1: (612)296-0334
Telephone #2: (612)296-2286
Assessment Date: January 2
Notification Date: Minimum of 10 days before Board review
Tax Bill Payment Date: May 15; October 15
Appeal Grievance Period: Prior to Local Board meeting (may vary)
Revaluation Period: 4 years
Personal Property Tax? No
Homestead Exemption? Yes

PROPERTY TAX APPEAL LEVELS

Level 1: Informal meeting with assessor
Level 2: Local Board of Review
Level 3: County Board of Equalization
Level 4: Minnesota Tax Court
Level 5: State Supreme Court

Notes: Appeals must be made by the taxpayer or an attorney. Property consultants may not appear for a taxpayer in appeal proceedings.

MISSISSIPPI

Agency Name: Property Tax Bureau
Mississippi State Tax
Commission
P.O. Box 960
Jackson, MS 39205-0960
Telephone #1: (601)359-1076
Assessment Date: January 1
Notification Date: Varies by county
Tax Bill Payment Date: February 1; August 1
Appeal Grievance Period: 1st Monday in July through 1st Monday in August
Revaluation Period: 1 year
Personal Property Tax? Yes
Homestead Exemption? Yes

PROPERTY TAX APPEAL LEVELS

Level 1: Informal meeting with assessor
Level 2: County Board of Supervisors
Level 3: Circuit Court of the County
Level 4: State Supreme Court

MISSOURI

Agency Name: State Tax Commission of
        Missouri
        621 East Capitol Avenue
        P.O. Box 146
        Jefferson City, MO 65102-0146
Telephone #1: (314)751-2414
Assessment Date: January 1
Notification Date: Varies
Tax Bill Payment Date: December 31
Appeal Grievance Period: Varies
Revaluation Period: 2 years
Personal Property Tax? Yes
Homestead Exemption? No

PROPERTY TAX APPEAL LEVELS

Level 1: Informal meeting with assessor
Level 2: Board of Equalization
Level 3: State Tax Commission
Level 4: Circuit Court System
Level 5: State Supreme Court

Notes: Property-tax consultants are not permitted to represent taxpayers at the State Tax Commission (but are permitted to do so at the local Board of Equalization).

MONTANA

Agency Name: State of Montana
        Department of Revenue
        Property Assessment Division
        Mitchell Building
        Helena, MT 59620
Telephone #1: (406)443-0811
Assessment Date: January 1
Notification Date: April 15
Tax Bill Payment Date: November 30; May 31
Appeal Grievance Period: Until 30 days after receiving notice
Revaluation Period: 5 years
Personal Property Tax? Yes
Homestead Exemption? Yes

PROPERTY TAX APPEAL LEVELS

Level 1: Informal meeting with assessor
Level 2: County Tax Appeals Board
Level 3: State Appeals

Level 4: District Court
Level 5: State Supreme Court

NEBRASKA

Agency Name: State of Nebraska
        Department of Revenue
        Property Tax Division
        P.O. Box 94818
        Lincoln, NE 68509
Telephone #1: (402)471-5729
Assessment Date: January 1
Notification Date: April 1
Tax Bill Payment Date: Varies by county
Appeal Grievance Period: April 1 through April 30
Revaluation Period: 1 year
Personal Property Tax? Yes
Homestead Exemption? Yes

PROPERTY TAX APPEAL LEVELS

Level 1: Informal meeting with assessor
Level 2: County Board of Equalization
Level 3: District Court
Level 4: State Board of Equalization

NEVADA

Agency Name: Nevada Department of Taxation
        Division of Assessment Standards
        Capitol Complex
        1340 South Curry Street
        Carson City, NV 89710-0003
Telephone #1: (702)687-4840
Assessment Date: January 1
Notification Date: January 1
Tax Bill Payment Date: Quarterly—June; October; January; March
Appeal Grievance Period: January 1 through 15
Revaluation Period: 5 years
Personal Property Tax? Yes
Homestead Exemption? Yes

PROPERTY TAX APPEAL LEVELS

Level 1: Informal meeting with assessor
Level 2: County Board
Level 3: State Board of Equalization
Level 4: Supreme Court

NEW HAMPSHIRE

Agency Name: State of New Hampshire
Department of Revenue
Administration
61 South Spring Street
P.O. Box 457
Concord, NH 03302-0457

Telephone #1: (603)271-2687
Telephone #2: (603)271-2191
Assessment Date: April 1
Notification Date: Varies by town
Tax Bill Payment Date: 30 days after notice of tax
Appeal Grievance Period: Local assessor: 2 months from receipt of tax
Revaluation Period: Varies by town
Personal Property Tax? No
Homestead Exemption? No

PROPERTY TAX APPEAL LEVELS

Level 1: Informal meeting with assessor
Level 2: Board of Tax and Land Appeals
Level 3: Superior Court
Level 4: State Supreme Court

Notes: If local assessor denies appeal, taxpayer has 8 months in which to appeal to either the Board of Tax and Land Appeals or the Superior Court.

NEW JERSEY

Agency Name: State of New Jersey
Division of Taxation, Department of the Treasury
Policy and Planning Section
50 Barrack Street–CN 251
Trenton, NJ 08646

Telephone #1: (609)292-7974
Assessment Date: October 1
Notification Date: None
Tax Bill Payment Date: February 1; May 1; August 1; November 1
Appeal Grievance Period: June 15 through August 15
Revaluation Period: Varies
Personal Property Tax? Yes
Homestead Exemption? Yes

PROPERTY TAX APPEAL LEVELS

Level 1: Informal meeting with assessor
Level 2: County Board
Level 3: Tax Court
Level 4: Appellate Division
Level 5: State Supreme Court

Notes: Property-tax consultants are not permitted to directly represent a property owner in an appeal. Corporations must be represented by a New Jersey Attorney

NEW MEXICO

Agency Name: State of New Mexico
Taxation and Revenue Department
Property Tax Division
P.O. Box 630
Santa Fe, NM 87509-0630

Telephone #1: (505)827-0700
Assessment Date: January 1
Notification Date: April 1
Tax Bill Payment Date: November 10; April 10
Appeal Grievance Period: 30 days from notification
Revaluation Period: 2 years
Personal Property Tax? Yes
Homestead Exemption? Yes

PROPERTY TAX APPEAL LEVELS

Level 1: Informal meeting with assessor
Level 2: County Valuation Protests Board or District Court
Level 3: State Court of Appeals
Level 4: State Supreme Court

Notes: Any authorized person may represent a taxpayer at board Appeals. All taxpayers appealing at the County Valuation Board are mailed a booklet describing appeal procedures in detail.

NEW YORK

Agency Name: State of New York
Division of Equalization and Assessment
Sheridan Hollow Plaza
16 Sheridan Avenue
Albany, NY 12210-2714

Telephone #1: (518)474-1700

Assessment Date: January 1, based on ownership and condition on March 1

Notification Date: Varies by municipality

Tax Bill Payment Date: Varies by municipality

Appeal Grievance Period: Varies by municipality, but usually is the

Revaluation Period: Varies by municipality (not mandated by state)

Personal Property Tax? No

Homestead Exemption? Yes, for low-income senior citizens and veterans

PROPERTY TAX APPEAL LEVELS

Level 1: Informal meeting with assessor

Level 2: Local Board of Assessment Review

Level 3: Small Claims Assessment Review

Level 4: State Supreme Court

Notes: Any designated person may represent a taxpayer before the Board of Assessment Review or Small Claims Assessment Review.

NORTH CAROLINA

Agency Name: North Carolina Department of Revenue
Property Tax Division
P.O. Box 871
Raleigh, NC 27602

Telephone #1: (919)733-7711

Assessment Date: January 1

Notification Date: August 31

Tax Bill Payment Date: September 1; January 5th

Appeal Grievance Period: 1st Monday in April through 1st Monday in May

Revaluation Period: 8 years

Personal Property Tax? Yes

Homestead Exemption? Yes, for elderly and disabled only

PROPERTY TAX APPEAL LEVELS

Level 1: Informal meeting with assessor

Level 2: County Board of Equalization

Level 3: State Property Tax Commission

Level 4: Court of Appeals

Level 5: State Supreme Court

Notes: Appeal levels above County Board of Equalization require that the taxpayer or attorney present appeal (no tax consultants).

NORTH DAKOTA

Agency Name: State Supervisor of Assessments
Office of State Tax Commissioner
600 East Boulevard Avenue
State Capitol Building
Bismarck, ND 58505-0599

Telephone #1: (701)224-3127

Telephone #2: (701)224-2770

Assessment Date: February 1

Notification Date: 10 days prior to Local Board of Equalization meeting

Tax Bill Payment Date: January 1 or March 1 and October 15

Appeal Grievance Period: at meeting of Local Board of Equalization

Revaluation Period: 1 year

Personal Property Tax? No

Homestead Exemption? Yes, for disabled or over age 65

PROPERTY TAX APPEAL LEVELS

Level 1: Informal meeting with assessor

Level 2: Local Board of Review

Level 3: County Board of Commissioners

Level 4: State Board of Equalization

Notes: An agent may represent taxpayer in tax appeals.

OHIO

Agency Name: Department of Taxation
Tax Equalization Tax Division
State Office Tower
P.O. Box 530, Floor 21
Columbus, OH 43266-0030

Telephone #1: (614)466-5744

Assessment Date: January 1

Notification Date: December 31

Tax Bill Payment Date: December 31; June 20

Appeal Grievance Period: Until March 31

Revaluation Period: 6 years

Personal Property Tax? Yes

Homestead Exemption? Yes

PROPERTY TAX APPEAL LEVELS

Level 1: Informal meeting with assessor

Level 2: County Board of Revision

Level 3: Board of Tax Appeals or County Court of Common Pleas

Level 4: Supreme Court or Court of Appeals

Notes: Only taxpayer or attorney may make appeals at levels higher than County Board of Revision.

OKLAHOMA

Agency Name: Oklahoma Tax Commission
Ad Valorem Tax Division
M. C. Connors Building
2501 N. Lincoln Boulevard
Oklahoma City, OK 73194-0003

Telephone #1: (405)521-3178

Assessment Date: January 1

Notification Date: Varies between April and May

Tax Bill Payment Date: December 31; January 30

Appeal Grievance Period: Until 20 days after mailing of notice

Revaluation Period: 1 year

Personal Property Tax? Yes

Homestead Exemption? Yes

PROPERTY TAX APPEAL LEVELS

Level 1: Informal meeting with assessor

Level 2: County Board of Equalization

Level 3: District Court

Level 4: Supreme Court

OREGON

Agency Name: Oregon Department of Revenue
Revenue Building
955 Center Street, N.E.
Salem, OR 97310

Telephone #1: (503)378-3022

Telephone #2: (503)378-3738

Assessment Date: July 1

Notification Date: October 25

Tax Bill Payment Date: November 15

Appeal Grievance Period: October 25 through December 31; and July 1 through July 15

Revaluation Period: 6 years

Personal Property Tax? Yes, on property used for business and mobile homes

Homestead Exemption? No

PROPERTY TAX APPEAL LEVELS

Level 1: Informal meeting with assessor

Level 2: County Board of Equalization and/or Board of Ratio Review

Level 3: Department of Revenue or Tax Court: Small Claims Division

Level 4: Tax Court

Level 5: State Supreme Court

Notes: Only licensed real estate brokers and state certified or licensed appraisers may act as property-tax consultants before the Department of Revenue in appeal proceedings.

PENNSYLVANIA

Agency Name: There is no state-level property-tax administration. All property-tax matters are handled at county level.

Assessment Date: Varies by county

Notification Date: Varies by county

Tax Bill Payment Date: Varies by county

Appeal Grievance Period: Varies by county

Revaluation Period: Varies by county

Personal Property Tax?

Homestead Exemption?

PROPERTY TAX APPEAL LEVELS

Level 1: Informal meeting with assessor

Level 2: Board of Assessment Appeals

Level 3: County Court of Common Pleas

RHODE ISLAND

Agency Name: Supervisor of Tax Equalization
Department of Administration
Office of Municipal Affairs
1 Capital Hill
Providence, RI 02908-5873

Telephone #1: (401)277-2885

Assessment Date: December 31

Notification Date: Varies by city or town, usually quarterly

Tax Bill Payment Date: Varies by city or town, usually quarterly

Appeal Grievance Period: Extends until 3 months after tax bill if bill

Revaluation Period: 10 years, but historically has often been extended

Personal Property Tax? Yes

Homestead Exemption? Yes, but only in Providence and Woonsocket

PROPERTY TAX APPEAL LEVELS

Level 1: Informal meeting with assessor
Level 2: Board of Assessment Review
Level 3: Superior Court

Notes: Taxpayer may be represented by agent in tax appeals. State exercises very little oversight of local property-tax administration.

SOUTH CAROLINA

Agency Name: South Carolina Tax Commission
Property Division
P.O. Box 125
Columbia, SC 29214

Telephone #1: (803)737-4485

Assessment Date: December 31

Notification Date: July 1

Tax Bill Payment Date: January 15

Appeal Grievance Period: Until 30 days following notice of assessment

Revaluation Period: 3 to 4 years, depending upon Sales/Ratio study.

Personal Property Tax? Yes (excluding personal property in a home).

Homestead Exemption? Yes, for elderly, disabled, and other groups.

PROPERTY TAX APPEAL LEVELS

Level 1: Informal meeting with assessor
Level 2: County Tax Assessor
Level 3: County Board of Tax Appeals
Level 4: South Carolina Tax Commission
Level 5: County Court

Level 6: State Supreme Court

Notes: Contact Taxpayer Rights Advocate, S.C. Tax Commission, P.O. Box 125, Columbia, SC 29214 for consumer tax information.

SOUTH DAKOTA

Agency Name: South Dakota Department of Revenue
Division of Property Taxes
700 Governors Drive
Pierre, SD 57501-2276

Telephone #1: (605)773-3311

Assessment Date: January 1

Notification Date: 2 weeks prior to April meeting of Local Board

Tax Bill Payment Date: May 1; November 1

Appeal Grievance Period: Prior to adjournment of Local Board

Revaluation Period: 1 year

Personal Property Tax? No

Homestead Exemption? Yes

PROPERTY TAX APPEAL LEVELS

Level 1: Informal meeting with assessor
Level 2: Local Board of Equalization and Review
Level 3: County Board of Equalization
Level 4: State Board of Equalization
Level 5: Circuit Court of the County

TENNESSEE

Agency Name: State Board of Equalization
505 Deadrick Street
Suite 1400
Nashville, TN 37243-0280

Telephone #1: (615)741-4883

Assessment Date: January 1

Notification Date: Prior to County Board meeting

Tax Bill Payment Date: October 1 through February 28 (some local exceptions)

Appeal Grievance Period: 45 days following County Board notice

Revaluation Period: 2 years

Personal Property Tax? Yes, for business property only

Homestead Exemption? Yes (for low-income elderly and disabled only)

PROPERTY TAX APPEAL LEVELS

Level 1: Informal meeting with assessor
Level 2: County Board of Equalization
Level 3: State Board of Equalization
Level 4: Chancery Court
Level 5: Court of Appeal
Level 6: Supreme Court

Notes: Property-tax consultants must be "qualified and registered with state board."

TEXAS

Agency Name: State Comptroller of Public
Accounts
Property Tax Division
4301 Westbank Drive
Building B, Suite 100
Austin, TX 78746-6565
Telephone #1: (512)329-7901
Assessment Date: January 1
Notification Date: May 15
Tax Bill Payment Date: January 31
Appeal Grievance Period: Before June 1
Revaluation Period: Varies by county, but usually 3 years
Personal Property Tax? Yes
Homestead Exemption? Yes

PROPERTY TAX APPEAL LEVELS

Level 1: Informal meeting with assessor
Level 2: Chief Appraiser
Level 3: Appraisal Review Board
Level 4: District Court
Notes: Personal property-tax is at local option for nonincome-producing personal property.

UTAH

Agency Name: Utah State Tax Commission
Property Tax Division
Heber M. Wells Building
160 East Third South
Salt Lake City, UT 84134
Telephone #1: (801)530-6177
Assessment Date: January 1

Notification Date: Varies by county, often July 22
Tax Bill Payment Date: Due by November 30
Appeal Grievance Period: 30 days after notice of valuation mailed
Revaluation Period: Varies by county
Personal Property Tax? Yes
Homestead Exemption? Yes, for primary residence

PROPERTY TAX APPEAL LEVELS

Level 1: Informal meeting with assessor
Level 2: County Board of Equalization
Level 3: State Tax Commission
Level 4: District Court
Level 5: State Supreme Court

Notes: Property-tax consultants must be Utah registered or certified appraisers in order to represent taxpayers in property-tax appeals.

VERMONT

Agency Name: State of Vermont
Department of Taxes
Division of Property Valuation
and Review
43 Randall Street
Waterbury, VT 05676
Telephone #1. (802)241-3500
Assessment Date: April 1
Notification Date: Varies
Tax Bill Payment Date: Varies
Appeal Grievance Period: Varies
Revaluation Period: 1 year
Personal Property Tax? Yes
Homestead Exemption? Yes

PROPERTY TAX APPEAL LEVELS

Level 1: Informal meeting with assessor
Level 2: Listers Grievance
Level 3: Board of Civil Authority
Level 4: State Board of Appraisers or Superior Court (but not both)
Level 5: State Supreme Court

Notes: Any authorized person may represent a taxpayer at appeals.

VIRGINIA

Agency Name: State of Virginia
Department of Taxation
Property Tax Division
P.O. Box 1-K
Richmond, VA 23201

Telephone #1: (804)367-8020
Assessment Date: Varies
Notification Date: Varies
Tax Bill Payment Date: Varies
Appeal Grievance Period: Varies
Revaluation Period: Varies
Personal Property Tax? Yes
Homestead Exemption? No

PROPERTY TAX APPEAL LEVELS

Level 1: Informal meeting with assessor
Level 2: Local Board of Equalization
Level 3: Circuit Court

Notes: Notarized agency authorization required in order for property-tax consultants to represent taxpayers in appeals.

WASHINGTON

Agency Name: State of Washington
Department of Revenue
Property Tax Division
General Administration Building
Olympia, WA 98504-0090

Telephone #1: (206)753-5503
Assessment Date: January 1
Notification Date: Varies
Tax Bill Payment Date: April 30; October 31
Appeal Grievance Period: July 1, or until 30 days after mailing of bills
Revaluation Period: Varies by county
Personal Property Tax? Yes
Homestead Exemption? Yes, for senior citizen and disabled persons

PROPERTY TAX APPEAL LEVELS

Level 1: Informal meeting with assessor
Level 2: County Board of Equalization
Level 3: State Board of Tax Appeals
Level 4: Superior Court

Notes: Any designated person may represent taxpayer in property-tax appeals.

WEST VIRGINIA

Agency Name: State of West Virginia
State Assessor's Office
409 Virginia Street East
Charleston, WV 25301

Telephone #1: (304)357-0250
Assessment Date: July 1
Notification Date: September 1
Tax Bill Payment Date: July 1
Appeal Grievance Period: February 1 through February 28
Revaluation Period: 3 years
Personal Property Tax? Yes
Homestead Exemption? Yes

PROPERTY TAX APPEAL LEVELS

Level 1: Informal meeting with assessor
Level 2: State Board of Equalization

WISCONSIN

Agency Name: State of Wisconsin
Bureau of Property Tax
P.O. Box 8933
Madison, WI 53708

Telephone #1: (608)266-1507
Assessment Date: January 1
Notification Date: Varies by county
Tax Bill Payment Date: January 31; July 31
Appeal Grievance Period: 2nd Monday in May through 2nd Monday in June
Revaluation Period: 4 years
Personal Property Tax? Yes
Homestead Exemption? Yes

PROPERTY TAX APPEAL LEVELS

Level 1: Informal meeting with assessor
Level 2: Board of Review
Level 3: State Board of Assessors
Level 4: Wisconsin Tax Appeals Commission
Level 5: Circuit Court
Level 6: Court of Appeals

WYOMING

Agency Name: State of Wyoming
Department of Revenue and
Taxation
122 West 25th Street
Cheyenne, WY 82002

Telephone #1: (307)777-7961
Telephone #2: (307)777-5287
Assessment Date: February 1
Notification Date: May
Tax Bill Payment Date: November 1; May 1
Appeal Grievance Period: Until 30 days following notification
Revaluation Period: 1 year

Personal Property Tax? Yes
Homestead Exemption? No

PROPERTY TAX APPEAL LEVELS

Level 1: Informal meeting with assessor
Level 2: County Board of Equalization
Level 3: State Board of Equalization
Level 4: District Court
Level 5: State Supreme Court

Notes: Contact Wyoming Taxpayer Association, 2424 Pioneer Ave., Suite 200, Cheyenne, WY 82001, Tel:(307)635-8761 for additional property-tax help information.

Property Data Forms and Checklists

Appendix B contains the following forms and checklists for your use:

Form 1. Assessor's Office Checklist
Form 2. Tax Appeal Checklist
Form 3. Checklist of Assessing Errors
Form 4. Comparable Sales
Form 5. Cost Approach Worksheet
Form 6. Sales/Assessment Ratio

FORM #1: ASSESSOR'S OFFICE CHECKLIST

DIRECTIONS:

Use this form to record important information about the assessing office, property records and local property tax appeal procedures in your area.

Property address: _____

Property map and lot number: _____

Assessed value for year_____: Land $_____ Bldg. $_____ Total $

Assessor's name _____

Assessor's mailing address _____

_____

Assessor's telephone number:_____

1. Tax bill No._____ Date payment made?_____

2. Assessment date_____

3. Bill payment due date(s)_____

4. Assessment notification date_____

5. Grievance period begins?_____

6. Last date to file grievance?_____

7. Copy of tax abatement application received?_____

8. Application for abatement filed?_____Date_____

9. Copy of higher level appeal procedures received?_____

10. Lower level appeal procedures satisfied so as to allow higher appeals later?_____

11. Is informal appointment with assessor possible to correct assessing errors prior to appeal period?

   _____

12. Copy of property record card received?_____

13. Other assessor records available for your use?:

   _____ List of property sales for district

   _____ Equalization study

_____ Assessing manual

_____ Cost manual

_____ Sales / assessment ratio study

_____ Taxpayer guides

14. Exemptions which you are eligible for:

 A. _____

 B. _____

 C. _____

15. Application for exemption(s) submitted? _____ Date_____

16. Date of last property revaluation _____

17. Date of next property revaluation _____

18. *Assessed value* for the current tax year is _____% of fair market value for this class of property.

19. Are the following useable as evidence of an unfair assessment in your area?:

 Equalization studies _____

 Sales / assessment ratio studies _____

20. Are there any taxpayer organizations or other consumer groups which the assessing office recommends for additional help and guidance?

_____

NOTES:

FORM #2: TAX APPEAL CHECKLIST

DIRECTIONS:

Use this checklist to organize the information you need to collect before submitting your tax appeal.
Your written appeal should be complete and self contained. Include copies of everything that you are using to argue your case. The following items should be included if relevant to your appeal:

_____ 1) *Cover letter:* This should be a concise (one page is best) summary of the main reasons for your appeal of the assessment. It should list all supporting evidence such as photos, completed market value analysis etc. that are enclosed. It must include your own opinion of value for the property and should identify the property by address and map and lot number.

_____ 2) *Town/City Abatement Request Form:* Many jurisdictions require that your abatement request be made in writing on a particular form supplied by the assessor's office. Be sure to use this form if required even though you submit other written letters, evidence etc. with it. In some jurisdictions failure to do so will prevent a later appeal by the property owner at the Board of Review or higher levels. Retain a date stamped copy as proof of timely submission.

_____ 3) *Photographs:* Include photographs (color is best) of your home if possible. Provide front and back views, as well as views of particular defects and adverse factors if appropriate.
Photographs of comparable properties are desireable to assure the assessor that the homes chosen are in fact comparable to yours. Write the street address and the map/lot number on the back of all photographs to aid identification.

_____ 4) *Comparable Sales Form:* The form included with this guide is an excellent way to organize your comparable sales information. Submit as many copies as needed to describe all comparables. (You are free to reproduce all forms included with this guide for your own use.)

_____ 5) *Cost Approach Form:* If you have done a cost approach analysis or have verified the assessor's cost approach as shown on the property record card, include a copy of your calculations. Use the form included with this guide or one from a commercial cost manual if used.

_____ 6) *Sales/Assessment Ratio Analysis:* If you have obtained a sales/assessment ratio analysis from the state or county assessing office and wish to use it in your appeal, include highlighted copies of pertinent sections. If you have prepared your own study, use the form included with this guide to organize and present your findings.

_____ 7) *Equalization Study:* If one is available from the assessing authority for your area, include highlighted copies of relevant sections supporting your claim.

_____ 8) *Copy of Property Deed:* Include if legal description of property in the deed (particularly the land) varies greatly from the assessor's description.

_____ 9) *Copy of Property Record Card:* If you have found significant errors on the property record card it may be worthwhile to highlight them on a copy of the card. This is especially so at appeal levels higher than the assessor, since appeal boards often do not have easy access to these records.

_____10) *Copy of Tax Bill:* This will reflect the latest assessed value and the owner of record.

_____11) *Copy of Sales Contract:* If you recently purchased your home, use this to help document a purchase price if less than the assessor's conclusion of fair market value.

_____12) *Contractor's Statement of Costs:* If available for a newly purchased home, use to document construction cost of home and to support your cost approach value analysis.

_____13) *Appraisal:* If you recently had your home professionally appraised, submit a copy of the appraisal if it supports a lower than assessed value. The closer the appraisal date is to the assessment date for tax purposes, the more useful it will be.

_____14) *Condominium Master Plan:* If you are disputing the size of your condominium unit or the percentage of total ownership which your unit represents, this official document may be used to support your opinion of fact.

_____15) *Other Supporting Evidence:* Any other evidence you are using, such as expert testimony in support of your findings, or evidence of depreciating off site factors such as high unemployment or an over built supply of homes.

_____16) *Letter of Agency:* If you have contracted with a property tax consultant, many jurisdictions require that the consultant be authorized in writing to represent you. This may be so even if the consultant is only forwarding to the assessor information which you have supplied.

_____17) *All Local Procedures Complied With:* Obtain a copy of the local procedure for filing tax abatement requests and all further levels of tax appeals. Failure to comply with local filing procedures will often preclude consideration of your appeal at any level.

_____18) *Filing Fee:* Certain higher levels of appeal in some states require that a filing fee be included when submitting the appeal.

FORM #3: CHECKLIST OF ASSESSING ERRORS

DIRECTIONS:

Place a check mark next to the items below which you believe have contributed to an incorrect assessment of your property. Prepare and submit evidence to support items checked.

GENERAL ASSESSMENT ERRORS

_____ Property assessed at more than fair market value

_____ Property assessed at a higher percentage of market value than similar properties

_____ Recent sales price of your home is lower than assessor's fair market value opinion

_____ Property assessed the same as more valuable properties

ILLEGAL ASSESSMENTS

Check with assessor for particular laws in your area. The following list is typical of many jurisdictions.)

_____ Property assessed at more than fair market value or more than the percentage of fair market value allowed by law for the class of property.

_____ Amount of assessment increase is greater than allowed by law

_____ Property is assessed in wrong class (i.e. commercial rather than residential)

_____ Property is listed in wrong tax district

_____ Property owner is wrongly identified

_____ Exemptions not allowed to which owner was entitled

_____ Assessor did not rely upon the approach or approaches to value mandated by law, or ignored data which would support a lower assessment

_____ Assessor did not follow other procedures as specified in state approved assessing manual

_____ Assessor ignored laws (statutory or case law) regarding specific assessing doctrine

_____ Assessor did not actually visit the property to perform appraisal as required by law

_____ Assessor did not certify the tax roll by giving official notice of its completion, or failed to follow other procedures as prescribed by law in validating the tax roll

_____ Assessor did not notify owner of increased assessment as required by law

_____ Revaluation of properties did not adhere to prescribed mass appraisal techniques or did not satisfy accuracy requirements as set by law

_____ Personal property incorrectly identified as real property or vice versa

_____ Property was not assessed as of the official assessment date

_____ Assessor did not consider restrictions to property rights, such as easements or newly enacted zoning or health and safety codes

_____ Assessor or staff was grossly negligent in carrying out duties of his or her office

MECHANICAL ERRORS

Look for the following when reviewing property record cards:

1. Land Description

_____ Total land area incorrect or differs from deed description

_____ Amount of frontage incorrect

_____ Amount of useable land incorrect

_____ Total acreage correct, but unimproved land incorrectly assessed at improved site rate

_____ Portion of land previously sold still listed as part of the total parcel

_____ Easements or restrictions to land use not accounted for

2. Building Description

_____ Wrong age listed for structure

_____ Number of stories incorrect

_____ Type and quality of construction incorrect

_____ Square footage of living area incorrect

_____ Nonliving areas such as porch or garage are listed as living areas and computed at more expensive square foot rate

_____ Demolished structure not removed from tax roll

_____ Basement description incorrect as to size/finish

_____ Exterior finish and condition incorrectly described

_____ Type of roof and condition incorrectly described

_____ Items such as pool or deck listed where none exist

_____ Amount of depreciation listed is incorrect

_____ Heating/cooling systems incorrectly described

_____ Wrong utilities listed as available

_____ Obsolete features of building not accounted for

_____ Room described as finished is incomplete

_____ Bathroom fixtures obsolete

(continued)

FORM 3 *(continued)*

_____ Number of bathrooms incorrect

_____ Number of fireplaces incorrect

_____ Home class incorrect (listed as two family when it is really a single family home, for example)

3. Mathematical and Clerical Errors

_____ Computations shown on property record card are incorrect (i.e., area of building or land, depreciation figures, etc.).

_____ Figures incorrectly copied from assessor record's to tax bill

_____ Wrong map and lot number listed on tax bill, resulting in payment of tax on wrong property

_____ Incorrect building permit or sales deed information about your property recorded on property record card or other assessor records

_____ Land area computations on plat map were incorrectly copied to property record card or other assessor records

4. Depreciating On-Site Factors Not Previously Accounted For:

_____ Wet basements

_____ Roof in poor condition

_____ Foundation cracked

_____ Termite damage

_____ Radon contamination

_____ Heavy land erosion

_____ Substandard landscaping

_____ Contaminated or insufficient water supply

_____ Deed restrictions

_____ Inadequate utilities

_____ Leaking ceiling/walls

_____ Substandard electric wiring

_____ Substandard plumbing

_____ Substandard exterior

_____ Substandard interior

_____ Substandard floor plan

_____ Storm/fire damage not repaired

_____ Dry rot

_____ Inadequate insulation

_____ Substandard floor materials

_____ Septic tank problems

5. Depreciating Off-Site Influences Not Previously Accounted For:

_____ Poor site access

_____ Below standard neighborhood

_____ Heavy traffic on road

_____ Inadequate fire, police, schools, transportation

_____ Inadequate drainage

_____ High crime rate

_____ Rising unemployment in local area

_____ Large number of unsold homes on the market

_____ Government restrictions to land use

_____ Toxic waste dump found nearby

_____ Noxious fumes and smoke from nearby dump

_____ Neighborhood flooding

_____ Noise pollution (airport, highway, factory, etc.)

_____ Commercial/industrial zone borders your property

_____ Deserted, abandoned structures near your property

Other:

PROPERTY TAX EXEMPTIONS

The following is a list of common exemption categories, which will vary from district to district. Check with your assessor to see which you may qualify for. In most districts a property owner *must apply* for exemptions or they will not be granted, even if property or owner meets qualifications.

_____ Homestead exemption

_____ Religious group

_____ Non-profit group

_____ Charitable group

(continued)

FORM 3 *(continued)*

_____ Veteran

_____ Disabled veteran

_____ Spouse of deceased or disabled veteran

_____ Spouse of deceased or disabled police or fire fighter

_____ Children of deceased or disabled police or fire fighter

_____ Historical property

_____ Household items (personal property tax exemption)

_____ Low income household

_____ Solar or wind energy powered devices

_____ Other anti-pollution structures and equipment

_____ Property used partially for farm or agricultural use

_____ Senior citizen

_____ Old age homes

_____ Hardship cases

_____ Blind or other disability

_____ Orphaned minors

_____ Mobile homes

_____ Personal property located outside of the tax district

_____ Home business incentive exemptions

OTHER EXEMPTIONS IN YOUR AREA:

_____

_____

_____

_____

_____

FORM #4: COMPARABLE SALES

(NOTE: Unless otherwise noted, sales reflect all property rights, normal financing terms and arm's length transactions. For all other factors, make + or − dollar value adjustments in each row as appropriate.)

OWNER NAME(S): _____

_____

SUBJECT PROPERTY ADDRESS: _____

SUBJECT MAP AND PARCEL NUMBER: _____

	COMPARABLE ____		COMPARABLE ____		COMPARABLE ____	
1. Property Address						
2. Sale Price						
3. Date of Sale / + or −						
4. Location / + or −						
5. Home SQ/FT Size / + or −						
6. Number of Rooms / + or −						
7. Number of Baths / + or −						
8. Garage / + or −						
9. Pool / + or −						
10. Deck or Porch / + or −						
11. Basement / + or −						
12. Fireplace / + or −						
13. Other Features / + or −						
14. Age / + or −						
15. Condition / + or −						
16. Land / + or −						
FINAL ADJUSTED SALES PRICE						

FORM #5: COST APPROACH WORKSHEET

Owner Name(s):_____

Property Address:_____

*Property Map & Parcel Number:*_____

VALUE OF IMPROVEMENTS

AREA 1: Residence

1. _____ sq/ft × $_____ per sq/ft = $_____
   (Living area)   (Cost per sq/ft)   (Cost of living area)

AREA 2: Non-living area (garage, screened porched etc.)

1. _____ sq/ft × $_____ per sq/ft = $_____
   (nonliving area)   (Cost per sq/ft)   (Cost of nonliving area)

3. TOTAL of lines 2 and 3: $_____

4. Amounts for extra features:

   Fireplace $_____

   Pool $_____

   Patio $_____

   Other Special Features $_____

5. TOTAL of lines 3 and 4: (Replacement Cost New) $_____

6. Minus depreciation amount: $_____

7. Current Value of Improvement $_____

VALUE OF LAND

8. Value of Land $_____

9. TOTAL value of property (line 7 + line 8): $_____

FORM #6: SALES/ASSESSMENT RATIO

DIRECTIONS: Choose 15 to 25 homes that have sold within the past year. Fill in the selling price of each home, as well as the assessed value of each, according to ther ecords in the assessor's office. Divide the assessed value by the selling price of each home to get the assessment rate. Add the total of all the assessment rates (a), then divide by the total number of properties (B) to get the average assessment rate (C). Compare the average assessment rate with the rate that your home has been assessed at.

No.	Street Address	Assessed Value	Divided by	Sales Price	=	Assessment Rate
1						
2						
3						
4						
5						
6						
7						
8						
9						
10						
11						
12						
13						
14						
15						
16						
17						
18						
19						
20						
21						
22						
23						
24						
25						

A	TOTAL OF ALL ASSESSMENT RATES:	
B	TOTAL NUMBER OF PROPRTIES USED:	
C	AVERAGE SALES/ASSESSMENT RATIO (LINE "A" DIVIDED BY LINE "B")	

Glossary

Abatement The reduction of an assessed valuation after the initial assessment has been completed. An abatement sometimes only applies to the assessed valuation for a single tax year and must be applied for again in later years.

Acre A land measure equal to 43,560 ft^2.

Ad valorem A Latin phrase meaning "according to the value."

Ad valorem tax Real estate tax based on property value.

Appraisal An opinion of the value or utility of specified real property.

Appraisal report A written report presenting an appraiser's expert opinion as to the value of some real property.

Appraiser One who performs an appraisal.

Assessed value In ad valorem taxation, the value according to the tax rolls.

Assessment The official valuation of property for taxation.

Assessment date Point in time when the most recent valuation of all properties in a tax district become legally established.

Assessment manual A state guideline that directs assessors and other government officials in property-tax procedures.

Assessor One who values property for property-tax administration purposes.

Bundle of rights All rights conferred by ownership of property, including the rights to enter and use the property, sell it, lease it, or not use it at all.

Chattel Personal property.

Classified property-tax A method of ad valorem taxation in which the effective tax rate varies according to the classification of the property, e.g., commercial, residential, or industrial.

Comparables Similar properties used for comparison with a subject property in the valuation process.

Comparable sales method Method of determining the market value of a property by comparing the subject property with comparable properties that have sold recently in the same area.

Condominium Form of ownership in a multiunit structure with individual ownership of units and shared ownership of common areas.

Cost manual A manual showing construction costs of various kinds of structures, used to estimate the replacement or reproduction cost of a structure in the cost method of property valuation.

Cost method Method of determining the value of a property by estimating the cost to reproduce or replace a building based on local construction costs, deducting from the new construction costs any accrued depreciation on the existing structure and then adding the estimated land value.

Deed A written, legal document that conveys an estate or interest in real property.

Depreciation A loss in property value from any cause; the difference between the cost to reproduce or replace a building and the market value as of the appraisal date.

Easement The right to use, without ownership, a portion of an owner's property.

Eminent domain The right of government to take private property for public use after the payment of fair compensation.

Equalization A procedure in which differing assessment rates among tax districts are compared.

Escheat The reversion of private property to the state when the owner dies without a will.

Fee-simple estate Complete ownership of the "bundle of rights" (*see* Bundle of Rights).

Front foot A land measure equal to one foot in width taken along the road or water frontage of a property.

Government rectangular system Describes the location of real estate with respect to meridians and base lines.

Highest and best use The use of land which brings the greatest net monetary return over a period of time.

Homestead exemption A release from assessment of a portion of property-tax, or the application of a lower tax rate on property designated as a family homestead.

Improvement Any addition to land that enhances its value.

Income approach Method of determining the value of a property by dividing the amount of net income the property produces annually by an appropriate capitalization rate. Often used to value income-producing property.

Intangible property Property that represents value but that cannot be touched by the senses, e.g., stocks and bonds.

Legal description A description of real estate that is recognized and approved by law.

Lot and block system A legal description of a parcel of land using the parcel's lot and block numbers that appear on maps and plats of recorded subdivided land.

Market value The price that a willing buyer and a willing seller, both knowledgeable and under no pressure to act, would agree on.

Mass appraisal A formalized method of appraising large numbers of properties together.

Metes and bounds Mapping system that uses distances and angles from some point of beginning to describe a parcel of real estate.

Mill One-tenth of a cent; often used to express real estate tax rates.

Mill rate Dollars per thousand dollars of assessed value.

Multiplier A numerical factor that is applied to a unit cost to adjust it for local variables. Used in the cost method of property valuation.

Notification date Date when new assessments are made public.

Obsolescence The state of a property that has become less valuable and desirable for continued use due to either functional or external factors; a cause of depreciation.

Personal property Property that by its nature is moveable and tangible.

Personalty Personal property, as opposed to real property.

Plat map A map indicating the location and boundaries of individual properties.

Police powers The right of the government to protect the health, safety, and general welfare of the public.

Property-tax Tax levied on real or personal property.

Property-tax base The assessed value of all taxable property within a designated area, such as a tax district.

Real property The various interests and rights associated with ownership of real estate.

Replacement cost Cost to replace an improvement with one having similar utility, using new materials, at current prices.

Reproduction cost Cost to replace an improvement with an exact replica.

Right-of-way The right to pass over the land of another.

Sales-assessment ratio Used as a measure of the relationship between an assessed value and the market value. The ratio is figured by dividing the assessed value of a property by the selling price.

Site Raw land that has been improved in some fashion, making it useable for a particular purpose.

Site improvements Improvements to a parcel of land that enable it to be used for a specific purpose. Examples include sidewalks, utility hookups, drainage systems, and landscaping.

Situs The physical location of real estate; the taxable location of personal property.

Special assessment An assessment against real estate levied by a public authority to pay for specific public improvements such as sidewalks, sewers, etc.

Tax calendar A calendar identifying all important dates in the tax assessing process for a particular tax district.

Tax map A map, drawn to scale, showing the boundaries and locations of individual lots and parcels in a tax district.

Tax rate Usually a rate expressed in dollars of tax per thousand dollars of assessed value, less commonly as dollars of tax per hundred dollars of assessed value.

Tax roll The official list of all taxpayers in a certain district subject to property-tax, the assessed values of their properties, and the amount of taxes due.

Tax sale The sale of a taxpayer's property to collect outstanding taxes; conducted when the taxpayer has not redeemed the property within the statutory period by paying the taxes due.

Zoning The public regulation of permitted uses of real estate, exercised under the police power of the state.

Works Consulted

Ackerman, Stephen J.: "Real Estate Appraisals," *Consumers' Research*, February, 1989, pp. 16–18.

Akerson, Charles B.: *The Appraiser's Workbook*. Chicago: American Institute of Real Estate Appraisers, 1985.

American Appraisal Associates, Inc.: "Do You Have Enough Property Insurance?" *Consumers' Research*, August, 1989, pp. 27–31.

American Institute of Real Estate Appraisers: *The Appraisal of Real Estate*, 9th ed. Chicago: American Institute of Real Estate Appraisers, 1987.

"Appraising the Expert's Sense of Value," *U.S. News & World Report*, September 19, 1988, pp. 70–71.

California State Board of Equalization: *Property Tax Facts for Policy Makers Pamphlet No. 29*. Sacremento, CA, August, 1987.

Babcock, Henry A.: *Appraisal Principals and Procedures*. Washington DC: American Society of Appraisers, 1980.

Driscoll, Lisa: "Is This Any Way to Write a Budget?" *Business Week*, September 2, 1991, p.34.

Hammonds, Keith H., Howard Gleckman, Ronald Grover and Joseph Weber: "Pity the Poor Taxpayer—States and Cities Are Squeezing Ever Harder," *Business Week*, September 2, 1977 p. 32–34.

Himstreet, William C.: *Communicating the Appraisal: The Narrative Report*. Chicago: American Institute of Real Estate Appraisers, 1988.

Hof, Robert and Jonathan B. Levine: "The Quake May Shake More Taxes Out of Californians," *Business Week*, November 6, 1989 p.42.

Institute of Property Taxation: *Property Taxation*, ed. Jerrold F. Janata. Washington, DC: Institute of Property Taxation, 1987.

International Association of Assessing Officers: *Property Assessment Valuation*. Chicago: International Association of Assessing Officers, 1977.

Jeffe, Douglas and Sherry: "A Tax Cap—Proposition 13 Ten Years Later," *Current*, November 1988, pp. 20–23.

Ludy, Andrew: *Condominium Ownership, A Buyer's Guide*. Landing, N.J.: The Landing Press, 1982.

Marshall & Swift: *Residential Cost Handbook*. Los Angeles: Marshall & Swift. Looseleaf; Quarterly.

Miller, George H., and Kenneth W. Gilbeau: *Residential Real Estate Appraisal: An Introduction to Real Estate Appraising*. Englewood Cliffs, N.J.: Prentice-Hall, 1980.

Index

About the Authors

VINCENT CZAPLYSKI is an appraiser and property tax consultant who has advised commercial and residential property owners throughout New England.

LAWRENCE CZAPLYSKI, a licensed Florida realtor, is a technical writer and editor.